Better Homes and Gardens®

Home Offices

YOUR GUIDE TO PLANNING AND FURNISHING

Better Homes and Gardens® Books
Des Moines, Iowa

Better Homes and Gardens® Books
An imprint of Meredith® Books

Home Offices: Your Guide to Planning and Furnishing
Writer/Editor: John Riha
Contributing Editor: Benjamin W. Allen
Associate Art Director: Lynda Haupert
Designer: Michael Burns
Copy Chief: Angela K. Renkoski
Copy Editor: Steve Marlens
Proofreader: James Sanders
Electronic Production Coordinator: Paula Forest
Editorial Assistants: Susan McBroom, Karen Schirm, Barbara A. Suk
Design Assistant: Jennifer Norris
Production Director: Douglas M. Johnston
Production Manager: Pam Kvitne
Prepress Coordinator: Marjorie J. Schenkelberg

Meredith® Books
Editor in Chief: James D. Blume
Design Director: Matt Strelecki
Managing Editor: Gregory H. Kayko
Executive Shelter Editor: Denise L. Caringer
Vice President, General Manager: Jamie L. Martin

Better Homes and Gardens® Magazine
Editor in Chief: Jean LemMon
Executive Building Editor: Joan McCloskey

Meredith Publishing Group
President, Publishing Group: Christopher M. Little
Vice President and Publishing Director: John P. Loughlin

Meredith Corporation
Chairman of the Board: Jack D. Rehm
President and Chief Executive Officer: William T. Kerr
Chairman of the Executive Committee: E. T. Meredith III

Cover photograph: Windows and efficient built-ins make going to work in this airy home office a pleasure. The essentials include window shades to reduce glare and filter light and a charming but practical roll-around chair. Photograph by D. Randolph Foulds.

Photographs: © Kenneth Rice Photography: page 28. © Eric Roth: pages 33, 71, 94, 95 (top), 104. Ed Gohlich: pages 58, 59. Hopkins Associates: pages 62, 63. Andy Lyons: pages 69, 109 (bottom).

Interior design: Paula Hart: pages 62, 63.

All of us at Better Homes and Gardens® Books are dedicated to providing you with information and ideas you need to enhance your home. We welcome your comments and suggestions about this book on home offices. Write to us at: Better Homes and Gardens Books, Do-It-Yourself Editorial Department, RW–206, 1716 Locust St., Des Moines, IA 50309–3023.

Contents

About This Book

This book is for the ever-growing number of Americans who have come to appreciate the idea of setting aside office space in the familiar comfort of their own homes. It is divided into five phases that guide you through the process of planning a home office. The first three phases help you envision your needs, determine the best location for your office, and anticipate upgrades to your home's electrical and mechanical systems. The last two phases offer advice on furnishing your office for a degree of comfort, efficiency, and style that will make you look forward to every workday. Following the last phase is a list of manufacturers, mail order firms, and associations that may aid you in planning and furnishing your home office.

PHASE 1: EVALUATING YOUR NEEDS

The Home Office

American homes are changing to include a comfortable place to work.

If you're thinking of creating an office in your home, you're in good company. In fact, more than 45 million Americans currently work at least part time from their homes, and more than 12 million work full time. Millions more have created distinct spaces for paying bills, keeping track of finances and investments, doing homework, and pursuing their hobbies.

The personal computer is part of this evolution. With its capacity to store volumes of documents in a tiny space and its ability to communicate with other computers anywhere in the world, the personal computer is helping to change the idea of what an office should be. Low-cost fax machines and copiers have made the home office efficient and productive. Many of us with full-time jobs can now work at least part of the week without leaving home.

This change in the way we do business and the way we live is having a profound effect on the way we organize our living spaces. Although many plans for new homes now include spaces designated specifically as home offices, most existing homes do not. That leaves rearranging or remodeling as the best ways to create an office within the home. Some solutions—such as converting a spare bedroom into an office—are straightforward, but others require much more ingenuity and foresight.

A well-planned home office is more than just a nice-looking space. It should be an organized environment that encourages creativity, aids productivity, and helps you get the most out of your workday. It should be a place you enjoy coming to regularly and one that is designed with your health and well-being in mind. A home office also can add value to your home when you sell it. If you remodel previously unused space, it means you have provided another living area that a buyer easily can convert to any use.

➤ *Even though the furnishings are simple, architecturally interesting features, such as the round window and the gable-vaulted ceiling, in this upper-level home office create an inspirational place to work. Around the corner, built-in bookshelves store reference materials.*

Level of Professionalism

A preliminary step in planning your home office involves considering what you hope to accomplish there. You must decide how professional it must look, and that depends on how much time you spend there and in what capacity. Common home office users include:

☐ Self-employed, full-time entrepreneurs with regular business clients

☐ Self-employed, full-time entrepreneurs with no clients

☐ Part-time telecommuters with access to a regular office or place of business at another location

☐ Part-time entrepreneurs

☐ Homeowners who simply desire a separate, distinct place to pay bills, file information, and complete correspondence

Each of these users has different home office needs for space, accessibility, flexibility, and location within the home. Individual needs also can vary widely. For example, someone who works full time for a corporation might generate a second income at home by spending an hour or two each evening designing clothes. That person would need a great deal of space for shelves, cutting tables, and a computer to help create designs and track expenses. A full-time, self-employed sales representative, however, also would need a home office but would spend relatively little time at home behind a desk. Evaluating your specific needs is crucial to designing a home office that works for you.

Establishing Boundaries

It is important to determine to what extent your office must be separated from your everyday home life. Some people have little difficulty integrating the hubbub of children, pets, and the occasional plumbing crisis into their home-based work lives. Others require strict separation from distractions, even when they're just balancing the family checkbook. Once you have a clear idea of whether you must separate your work from your family life or whether you can weave the two

together, you can design and locate your home office accordingly.

For privacy, situate your office as far away from in-home traffic patterns as possible. Basements, attics, or garages are good candidates for conversions. Acoustic insulation in walls and ceilings blocks noise transmission, as does a closed door. If it is not possible to have your home office in a separate room, you can create privacy with screens or bookshelves. Two phone lines—one for family use and one for business—are recommended. And then there's the human element: Simply talk with your family about your preference for privacy and establish some house rules.

■ *How much space is enough? This clothes designer's office, left, has a desk for tracking expenses and a big, light-filled shop for creating prototypes. The kitchen office, above, is in a remodeled closet that hides away when not in use.*

See Also:
☐ Insulating Against Noise, pages 70–73

Public Access

Your work may include regular visits from clients. If so, your home office will have special requirements. For one, its location should be readily accessible from the outside. A first-floor room on the side of your house that faces the street would make a good choice. Ideally, it also should have its own entrance to the outside that is clearly recognizable as the door to your office.

Be sure to provide clients with a place to hang coats and hats and, if necessary, a waiting area with comfortable seating. You'll also want a conference table with chairs or at least some extra seating near your desk. If you anticipate extended meetings, it would be wise to locate a bathroom near your office so clients won't have to wander through your home to use the facilities.

If clients will visit your home-based office, be sure it looks professional. Clients expect your office to be clean, well-organized, and pleasant. This applies to the exterior of your home as well as to the interior of your office. Walkways must be kept free of debris, old newspapers, and toys; steps and railings must be clean and in good repair. Your landscaping—shrubs, flower beds, and lawn—should be kept trimmed and healthy.

The costs of maintaining, repairing, and cleaning your home office may be tax-deductible business expenses. Always check with your accountant or tax adviser before claiming home office tax deductions.

See Also:
- Zoning Ordinances and Restrictions, page 10
- Tax Deductions for Home Offices, pages 12–13

▼ *A separate entrance is a must for a home-based architect with clients who regularly visit his attic office. The owner took advantage of the remodeling project to fill the gable end with windows.*

▲ *The full-time professional who works in this remodeled spare bedroom accommodates clients with a professional atmosphere and comfortable seating.*

Zoning Ordinances And Restrictions

Towns, cities, and villages may have specific ordinances governing the use of homes for business purposes. Many require a permit for a home office, particularly where there will be employees in addition to the homeowner or visiting clients. For the most part, such ordinances are designed to protect residential neighborhoods from unwanted traffic, parking problems, inappropriate signs, and noise.

Most towns or municipalities are divided into districts or zones. Each zone places restrictions on the uses of existing buildings and dictates what types of new buildings can be constructed, how they can be used, and even their height. One zone may limit a home-based business to no more than 20 percent of the total square footage of a residence; another zone may forbid home offices altogether. To complicate matters, several states also have laws governing home-based businesses. Many of these were enacted in the 1930s to prevent abusive labor practices, such as mandatory 12-hour work days. Be aware that these antiquated laws may still affect your ability to establish a home office.

It's important to remember that zoning ordinances vary widely from town to town. Before establishing your home office, check with your local planning and zoning commission about possible ordinances or laws governing your neighborhood. They can provide a zoning map and guidelines governing the use of real estate in each zone. It is always a good idea to seek the advice of a planning official to make sure you understand the guidelines completely.

Certain planned communities or condominium associations have covenants and bylaws that restrict the creation of home-based businesses and home offices. Make your intentions clear to the proper association officials before proceeding with your plans. Be aware, however, that getting the approval of a local association doesn't mean you will pass the zoning requirements of your municipality. You must check with all governing organizations before you proceed.

If local ordinances prevent you from establishing your home-based business or office, you might be able to apply for a variance. Check with local planning officials to determine the correct procedure. You might also want to consult an attorney who specializes in real estate law.

▶ *The owner of this house had to check local zoning ordinances to see if she could establish a home-based furnishings business and advertise her shop by placing a sign in the front yard.*

AMERICANS WITH DISABILITIES ACT

The Americans With Disabilities Act was created in the 1970s to make sure certain public buildings provided access for people with handicaps. In 1992, the ADA was amended to include any public facility where more than 15 people are employed. Most home offices are not governed by the ADA. However, you should consider voluntary compliance if you expect handicapped clients. In most cases, this means designing wheelchair ramps instead of stairs and doorways that are at least 36 inches wide. For more information, call the Center for Accessible Housing at 800/647-6777.

Insurance and Taxes

Whether you plan to use your office for part-time or full-time work, you should be aware of how it might affect your home finances, insurance, and tax obligations. Your attention to these matters will safeguard your home and business against loss and may provide certain tax benefits.

Insurance

If you are planning changes to your house to accommodate a home office, it's a good idea to review your homeowner's coverage with your insurance agent. This is especially true if you plan to convert an unused space, such as an attic or basement, into an office. These kinds of improvements might increase the value of your home substantially, and your homeowner's insurance should reflect that. Computers, printers, file cabinets, and other valuable office equipment and furnishings should be covered. If your homeowner's policy doesn't include these items, ask your agent about having them specifically included in your policy—an addition known as an insurance rider. Keep careful documentation of your purchases of equipment and furnishings. Some agents also recommend keeping a photographic record of items along with their serial numbers, dates of purchase, and cost in your safe-deposit box.

If you run a business from your home, you may need liability, business property, and disability insurance. Check with your agent to see if you can attach a rider to your homeowner's policy or buy a separate policy for these types of insurance.

Tax Deductions for Home Offices

If you are self-employed and use a home office as your principal place of business, you may be entitled to certain federal tax deductions. The tax

▲ *For insurance purposes, you should keep a complete record of your office supplies and equipment, including valuable ancillary items such as artwork and lamps.*

laws regarding use of a home for business are complex. It's always wise to seek the advice of a tax consultant who can help you manage your tax obligations and find the deductions to which you are entitled.

Generally, there are two kinds of deductions for the home office worker: business expenses and home office expenses. Business expenses are costs required for the operation of your business. Some of these include office supplies, postage, telephone service, advertising, furniture, and such equipment as copiers and computers. Check with your tax consultant or refer to IRS publications (listed below right) to see which expenses are allowed.

You may qualify for a deduction of expenses for the business use of your home. This deduction is a percentage of the annual cost of operating and maintaining your home. It is based upon the size of your office in relation to the size of the living area of your home. If you live in a 2,000-square-foot home with a 200-square-foot office, your office space is 10 percent of your home. Therefore, you may be entitled to deduct 10 percent of the annual costs of expenses, such as utilities, insurance, repairs, and property taxes.

The proliferation of home offices in the past few years has prompted IRS agents to pay closer attention to the home office deduction. To qualify, your home office must be used exclusively and regularly for business purposes and must be at least one of the following:

☐ Your principal place of business
☐ The location where you meet clients
☐ A separate structure from your house

Whether you meet these criteria is not always obvious. For example, self-employed plumbers who use home offices for billing and accounting may not qualify for the deduction because their "principal place of business" is usually someone else's home, not their own.

If you qualify for the home office deduction, be aware that there are tax obligations you may encounter. If you sell your home for more than you paid for it, you may be required to pay taxes on the profit. For example, if you sold your home for $20,000 more than you paid for it, but have

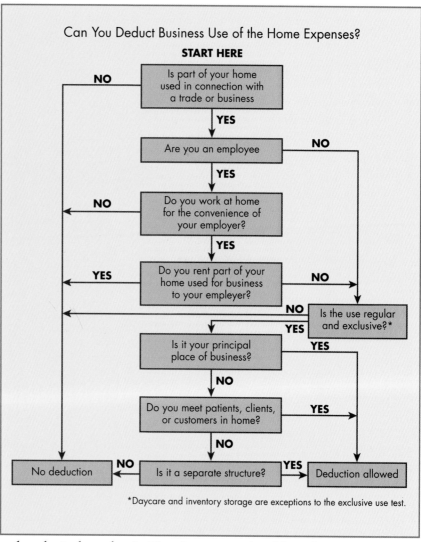

Can You Deduct Business Use of the Home Expenses?

*Daycare and inventory storage are exceptions to the exclusive use test.

▲ *This chart is reproduced from the Internal Revenue Service Publication 587: "Business Use of Your Home."*

been claiming a home office deduction of 10 percent annually, you may be liable for taxes on 10 percent of the profit, or taxes on $2,000. Consider this possibility when deciding whether to claim a home office deduction.

The Internal Revenue Service has publications to help homeowners and home-based business operators. IRS Publication 587, "Business Use of Your Home," helps you meet your tax obligations and claim the right deductions. To order this or other helpful publications, check your telephone book listings under "United States Government" for the nearest Internal Revenue Service office.

Finding Space In Your Home

Your home has many locations, both large and small, that can be perfect for your home office needs.

Your specific needs will dictate where you can place an office within your home. If your only task is part-time paperwork or studying, you may be able to fit a small desk, some shelves, and a reading lamp in an out-of-the-way location, such as a large closet. Or, consider using space within a particular room in such a way that it is unobtrusive or can be easily concealed. Cleverly designed furniture available in today's marketplace can masquerade as an armoire or entertainment center, but when it's opened, a full-fledged office set-up is revealed—complete with computer stand and storage shelves. Many people create work areas in their kitchens that include a desk, chair, and a telephone, then take advantage of nearby kitchen cabinets for storage of essential materials or equipment, such as fax machines.

If you need more space, consider appropriating a spare bedroom or converting a little-used den or dining room into an office. If you require an even more generously proportioned space, consider remodeling a basement or attic. Basements and attics offer plenty of privacy and are separated from normal household activities. But they require more planning and remodeling and, therefore, generally cost more than simpler conversions.

Another option is to create a brand new space for your home office. If you are planning to build a new home, you can custom-design your home office. Discuss your needs in detail with your architect or home planner. Even if you're not building an entire new home, you might consider adding onto your existing home or even building a small home office as a separate structure. Although constructing a separate structure requires that you become involved with basic house systems, such as electricity and heat, you will have the luxury of total separation between home and work environments.

Garage Conversions
☐ **Pros:** *The area over a garage provides a good amount of unused living space in a location separate from normal home life.*
☐ **Cons:** *Garage conversions usually require extensive, costly remodelings.*

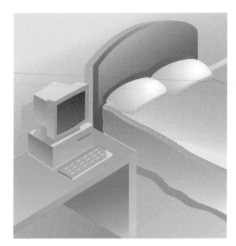

Master Bedrooms
☐ **Pros:** *A master bedroom is usually large enough to include a small office. This location generally is quiet during the day and out of the way of normal household activities.*
☐ **Cons:** *You'll have to sleep with your work nearby. You may have to find storage outside the room for work-related materials.*

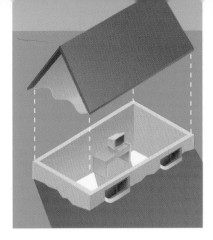

Basements

☐ **Pros:** *Basements are private and out of the way. Conversion of this space can add to your home's value. Basements often offer a generous amount of space.*

☐ **Cons:** *Basements can be cool, damp, and even lonely. Fresh air and light may be minimal. Low ceilings may contribute to a sense of claustrophobia.*

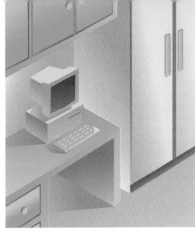

Kitchens

☐ **Pros:** *Kitchens are generally comfortable and well-lighted and make good locations for small offices or work centers. Existing cabinets can be used for storage of work-related materials.*

☐ **Cons:** *The kitchen is the hub of family activities, and it may be difficult to separate your work from the bustle of home life.*

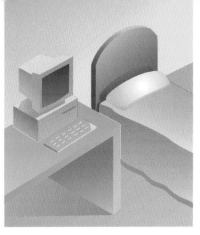

Spare Bedrooms

☐ **Pros:** *A spare bedroom is the easiest and most popular place to create a home office. It comes complete with electricity, lighting, a door for privacy, and a closet for storage. And it doesn't intrude on other living areas.*

☐ **Cons:** *You lose valuable space for overnight guests and for storage.*

Living, Dining, or Family Rooms

☐ **Pros:** *These spaces can accommodate desks and shelves, and there is usually a table nearby that can serve as an extra work surface.*

☐ **Cons:** *These are public areas within the home, and you will have to manage the conflict between work and home environments.*

Attics

☐ **Pros:** *Attic conversions generally offer privacy and plenty of space. Plus, there is the romance of being on the top floor with access to light and great views.*

☐ **Cons:** *Attic conversions may require structural changes to meet building codes. They may also require insulation, extension of heating and cooling systems, and cutting through the roof or gables if there are no windows.*

Separate Structures

☐ **Pros:** *Creates an independent, well-defined place for work that is private and quiet. Because it's new, it can be custom-designed.*

☐ **Cons:** *Zoning ordinances or local covenants may prohibit construction of separate structures. New construction and the extension of electrical and telephone services are relatively expensive.*

Spare Bedrooms

One of the easiest and most efficient ways to create a home office is to convert a spare room, such as a bedroom. A typical bedroom is between 110 and 160 square feet, big enough to accommodate a generous office that includes a desk and an office chair, file cabinets, shelves for books, and even space for a comfortable easy chair. As a bonus, the closet can serve as a storage area that keeps files out of sight.

A spare bedroom probably will have adequate window light; finished wall, ceiling, and floor surfaces; and enough electrical outlets to allow you to arrange your office machines as you want. If your office needs are modest, you may even be able to keep a twin bed, daybed, or sleeper couch that allows you to use the room for overnight guests. (Remember that using your office for any other purpose besides work will prevent you from claiming the space as a tax deduction.)

Converting a spare bedroom to office use probably will not affect your home's resale value, particularly if your house has four or five bedrooms. If you own a two- or three-bedroom home, however, you should consider its resale value before making any substantial alterations, such as installing built-in shelving, adding sound insulation, or changing window and door configurations. Changes that reduce the number of bedrooms may affect a potential buyer's willingness to purchase your home.

➤ *Built-in pine shelves and storage units were added around the generous windows when this 13×13-foot bedroom was converted to a home office. Knickknacks and family pictures keep the space from being too formal. A window seat helps create a cozy work environment.*

Spare Bedrooms

If you have the luxury of choosing which spare room can be your office, consider these environmental factors:

☐ Rooms with windows that face the street tend to be noisier than rooms on the opposite side of the house.

☐ Rooms that are located next to or over family rooms or the kitchen generally are noisier than other rooms.

☐ Rooms facing west are more prone to temperature fluctuations.

See Also:
☐ Insurance and Taxes, pages 12–13
☐ Insulating Against Noise, pages 70–73

▶ *You don't have to sacrifice a guest room to create a home office. Here a desk with a telephone, computer, fax machine, and storage coexists with a single bed. The stylish wall finish of this upper-level bedroom conversion keeps the space lighthearted for either use.*

▶ *One of the great benefits of a spare bedroom conversion is a closet for storage. This home office features a writing desk strategically placed beside a closet with built-in bookshelves for easy access to reference materials.*

Attics

Attics offer great potential for remodeling. They are often unused spaces that can be converted to quiet, private, generously proportioned home offices. Many attics can be architecturally interesting, too, with sloped ceilings, delightful nooks, and treetop views.

Attic conversions are not always easy, however. Ceilings may be too low, the area may be broken up by chimneys or vent stacks, and framing members, such as trusses or collar ties, may cut through the space. It may be difficult to reach the attic from below. Also keep in mind that an unfinished attic often seems much larger than when it's finished. Knee (or side) walls and flat ceilings in previously wide-open attics considerably diminish the room's finished proportions.

The first step in evaluating your attic's potential is familiarizing yourself with local building codes or consulting a building inspector or architect. Most building codes require that at least 50 percent of the floor area have a ceiling height of 7 feet, 6 inches. Codes may also require that knee walls be at least 5 feet high. Dormers may be allowed, but you should check your building code for specifics.

Headroom

In some cases, headroom requirements make an attic conversion impractical. For example, if your attic is lower than 7 feet, 6 inches at its ridge board (the peak of the roof framing), you won't be able to use the space without raising the entire roof—a major job. If your roof is framed with trusses—triangular or scissor-shaped framing members—you will not be able to use the space unless you reframe the entire roof. If your roof is not framed with trusses, it probably has collar ties—horizontal framing members that span pairs of rafters and help prevent the rafters from spreading apart. If the collar ties intrude on your plans for remodeling, it is possible they can be shortened and raised. However, because they play an important structural role, you will need to consult an architect or structural engineer before relocating collar ties.

If your roof is steep, the chances are the collar ties are located above the 7-foot, 6-inch level. If so, it may be possible to install drywall under the ties to create a flat ceiling over at least a portion of your attic office. With a flat ceiling, you may be able to add recessed lighting or even a ceiling fan. Be sure to insulate behind the drywall and to provide gable-end vents for this space to allow excess heat and moisture to escape.

If you prefer the look of a sloped ceiling all the way to the peak, leave the collar ties exposed, then insulate and finish the space between the rafters. You will need vents in the soffits under the eaves to prevent moisture and heat from building up underneath the roofing material. If the exposed collar ties aren't attractive, you can cover them with wood or drywall.

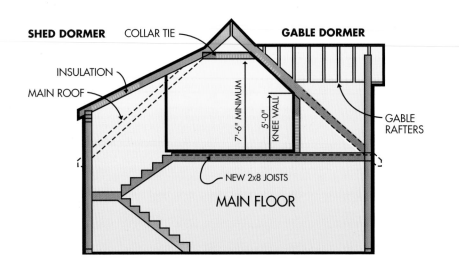

◀ *A remodeled attic usually will include several of the features depicted in this drawing. Dormers create more usable space and can bring lots of light into an otherwise dim space.*

▲ *Although only a 10×14-foot space, this attic office has great character and work space for two. A stylish partition wall, dressed up with moldings and leaded-* *glass windows, separates the work area from a small reading/relaxing nook with a window seat and rocking chair. Skylights add plenty of light.*

Floors

You'll have to check the structural strength of your attic's floor. The floor joists may not have been designed with the weight of people and office furnishings in mind. This is a job for a structural engineer or qualified architect. If your floor joists need strengthening, you probably will need to "sister" the old joists by adding new ones alongside the originals. If possible, use joists of the same dimension as the originals. If an engineer or architect specifies larger joists, remember that because the ceiling material for rooms below is attached to the bottom of the joists, you cannot add new, larger joists that will extend downward—only upward—raising the level of your attic's floor and shortening headroom. Make sure to take this into account.

If you open the floor to work on the joists, you have an excellent opportunity to insulate against noise. Fiberglass batts installed between the joists help reduce noise from rooms below. Where the floor will remain sealed, carpets also can help deaden sound.

Heating and Cooling

Even if you insulate between rafters and in the end walls, your attic undoubtedly will get quite warm in the summer. The temperature in an uninsulated attic can exceed 140 degrees. Even with insulation, you'll need to install a window-type air-conditioning unit or extend your home's air-conditioning system. If you extend your existing system, you'll have to find a way to bring ductwork to the attic. A heating and cooling contractor may be able to use an existing chase—a wall cavity built to channel mechanical systems through your home's interior. Otherwise, you will need to build one, and finding space for it can be tough. It's best to consult an expert.

Although your attic may be the warmest and most comfortable area of your house during the winter, there will be times when it undoubtedly will require a supplemental heating system. Electric baseboard or space heaters are simple solutions. The only requirement is an available electrical circuit that can handle the load. Consult a licensed electrician about the electrical needs of your new office.

Your attic should be fully insulated according to local building codes—most likely a value of R-30 in the ceiling and at least R-13 in the walls. If you are insulating between rafters, install a vapor barrier on the warm side of the room between the rafters and the drywall.

■ *There's a home office in this remodeled attic space—and a lot more. Comfortable furniture creates an inviting, casual family room. There's plenty of light, but it is carefully regulated by wooden blinds.*

Insulating batts should not fill the cavity between the rafters entirely—there must be an airspace above the insulation and vents in the eaves and near the ridge to promote air circulation.

Stairs

Getting to the attic comfortably often means enlarging an existing stair or adding a new one. This will affect the area below, so planning is important. Local building codes are specific about stair construction. Stairs are usually a minimum of 3 feet wide and 10 to 14 feet long. If you use an intermediate landing, allow about 8 feet of length on the lower level.

It's a good idea to plan stairways with a copy of the blueprints for your house in hand, if you have them. Otherwise, make accurate sketches of your home's floor plan and start with those. It often is best to start a stairway nearer one side of the house, letting the stairs flow up toward the

THE INSIDE STORY

The owner of this Boulder, Colorado, house was an advertising executive in Chicago until he decided to get away from it all and start his own consulting business. Working with an architect, the homeowner created a cheery, comfortable work space, *left*, on the third level of his home. The key to success is plenty of light, which enters through windows, skylights, and even French doors to a small balcony, *above*, with a view of the mountains. Soft, caramel-colored walls set off with crisp white trim enhance the feeling of spaciousness. The entrance to the attic is a stairway, *left top*, cleverly disguised behind a low partition wall in one corner of the office.

middle of the attic where the opening can be surrounded by a railing. Locating a stairway over an existing stairwell is one option. Or, consider starting the stairway in an existing closet. Pay close attention to where the stair will land in the attic, making sure sloping ceilings don't interfere with it. The minimum headroom required over a landing is typically 6 feet, 8 inches.

For a spiral stairway, you'll need a minimum diameter of 5 feet. However, building codes may require a larger stair in living areas. Keep in mind that spiral stairways make it difficult to carry up furniture and other large objects.

Dormers

To increase usable space, consider adding one or more dormers to your attic. A dormer creates a new, smaller roof over a portion of your attic and usually provides new sections of vertical walls where windows can be added. Dormers admit light and fresh air; they also can help solve remodeling problems, such as where to locate a stairway landing.

There are two basic types of dormers: gable-roof and shed. A gable-roof dormer has a peaked roof with a ridge at a right angle to the main roof. Ideally, the roof pitch of the gable dormer should match that of your house, and the dormer ridge should not rise above the height of the main ridge. On the interior, a gable-roof dormer often makes a small alcove that is perfect for a window seat, dresser, or even a small writing desk.

A shed dormer has a simple, sloped roofline that is flatter than the pitch of the main roof. This type of dormer can be almost as wide as the main roof. If you plan to shingle the dormer roof, remember that the minimum pitch required is usually 3 in 12, or 3 inches of vertical rise for every 12 inches of horizontal run. Any shallower pitch will require special roofing materials designed for flat roofs.

Adding a dormer requires cutting existing rafters and providing temporary supports. Framing techniques must conform to building codes, and the places where the existing roof has been cut will need to be sealed against the weather. All these are major considerations with significant consequences should something go wrong, and it is wise to consult a qualified con-

▶ *Furnished with a built-in desk, a comfortable overstuffed chair, and a cushioned seating ledge, this small attic office also makes a relaxing retreat.*

▼ *The stairway access takes up space, but the simple railing system visually keeps the office open. Skylights add brightness, and low shelving against knee walls puts every available inch to work.*

tractor, structural engineer, or architect before proceeding with your plans.

Skylights

Skylights bring light and fresh air into attic offices. Various types of factory-built skylights open manually or electronically and provide full or partial shading. Installation usually requires cutting at least one rafter to allow room for the skylight unit, and the opening must be reframed with headers according to building codes. The roofing material immediately surrounding the opening probably will have to be removed and replaced in such a way as to ensure a tight, weatherproof seal around the skylight. This is tricky, and poorly installed skylights often leak. Unless you have adequate remodeling experience, skylight installation is best left to licensed and bonded contractors who guarantee their work in writing.

Basements

Basements, like attics, are often large, relatively unused spaces. They are quiet and out of the way of household activity, and there is usually an existing stairway and easy access to electrical circuits that can provide the power for your lighting and office equipment. Converting an unused basement space into a finished living area almost certainly will increase your home's market value. According to the National Association of Home Builders, you are likely to recover 60 to 90 percent of the cost of remodeling your basement when you sell your home.

Although natural light and ventilation may be in short supply in your basement, remodeling can make the area completely livable. Before you begin, you'll need to evaluate your basement for adequate headroom and moisture problems. Careful planning will ensure your basement office stays dry and comfortable throughout the year.

▲ *A suspended ceiling system and sophisticated wall finishes add a touch of elegance to this sleek basement office. The built-in desk sits behind a raised counter that doubles as a buffet for entertaining.*

▼ *For the ultimate in comfort, install a new floor over your basement's concrete slab. You can finish the floor with carpet, tile, or even wood. A vapor barrier helps eliminate moisture concerns.*

▶ *New walls inside the old ones allow you to add insulation and drywall. Install a vapor barrier between the foundation and the studs.*

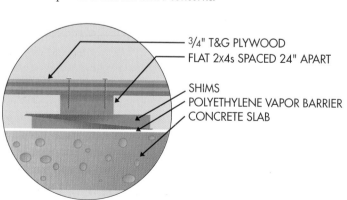

3/4" T&G PLYWOOD
FLAT 2x4s SPACED 24" APART
SHIMS
POLYETHYLENE VAPOR BARRIER
CONCRETE SLAB

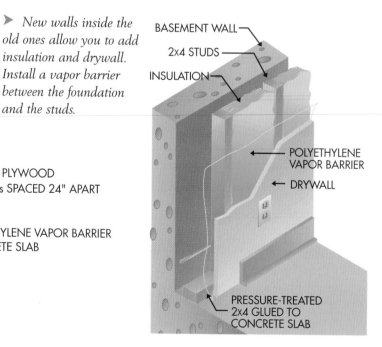

BASEMENT WALL
2x4 STUDS
INSULATION
POLYETHYLENE VAPOR BARRIER
DRYWALL
PRESSURE-TREATED 2x4 GLUED TO CONCRETE SLAB

Ceilings

When examining your basement for home office potential, one of the first things you'll notice is the tangle of pipes, wires, ducts, and framing that comprise the ceiling. If you'd like to hide this overhead confusion, there are two possibilities. The simplest is to camouflage the overhead mess by painting it all a single color. This works remarkably well and is inexpensive. Using a sprayer makes the job easier, but wear a mask designed to filter out harmful vapors while you're working. Because basements tend to be dark, you'll probably want to select a paint that is light in color. To enhance the effect, paint basement walls a contrasting color.

The second option is to install a false or suspended ceiling. A suspended ceiling is a lightweight metal grid designed to hold acoustic tile panels. The panels hide pipes, ducts, and joists, yet they are easily removed for maintenance. They also provide a measure of sound insulation from rooms above. For more effective sound insulation, staple fiberglass batts between the joists before installing the suspended ceiling. Most suspended ceiling systems also offer optional modular fluorescent light boxes that fit neatly into the grid for overhead lighting.

Remember that a suspended ceiling lowers headroom, and building codes dictate that ceilings must be 7 feet, 6 inches high in living areas. Your building inspector will enforce these height restrictions.

If you want your basement to have a more finished appearance, you may want to install drywall on the ceiling. Drywall can be nailed directly to the joists, as long as all pipes, wires, and ductwork run above the bottom of the joists. However, drywall effectively seals off mechanical systems in the ceiling, so it's a good idea to include removable access panels where you might need to service pipes and wires.

Moisture

Damp walls and floors—frequent problems in basements—usually are caused by moisture wicking through foundation walls or entering through cracks and other imperfections. The underlying cause of the problem is often inadequate drainage around the outside of your house. Your first line of defense is to make sure gutters are kept free of debris. Overflowing gutters cause water to pool on the ground near the foundation, soaking the soil and encouraging moisture to enter the basement. Downspouts should be long enough to channel water at least 6 feet out from foundation walls. Also, make sure the soil around your house is graded so water drains away from the foundation. The soil surface should slope ¼ inch per running foot for a distance of at least 6 feet from the foundation walls. Look for low spots where water pools; fill these with topsoil.

If your basement has a sump pump, consider adding a backup unit to handle overflow. If flooding is frequent, you might even consider providing an emergency generator for use during power outages. The generator helps protect your investment and provides peace of mind.

If your basement has few moisture problems, make sure it stays that way with periodic checks of the drainage conditions outside your home. Serious moisture problems may require the advice of an expert. Ask a qualified general contractor to recommend a waterproofing contractor.

Walls and Floors

For maximum comfort, it's a good idea to insulate basement walls, particularly if you live in a

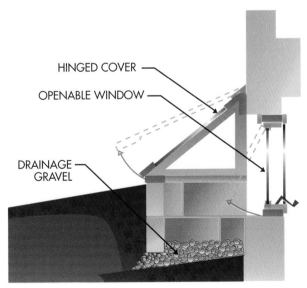

▼ *Window wells are one way to bring daylight and fresh air to below-grade home offices. A properly constructed window well includes adequate drainage and a hinged cover that keeps the well free of debris.*

HINGED COVER

OPENABLE WINDOW

DRAINAGE GRAVEL

northern climate, where the temperature of the soil in winter can slip below 50 degrees. To insulate, you'll need to construct simple 2×4 frame walls against your basement's concrete walls. These new walls add thermal insulation, provide a place to run electrical and telephone wires throughout your new office, and help reduce moisture problems. They also accept a variety of wall surface finishes.

The walls should have a pressure-treated bottom plate that is glued to the floor with construction adhesive. When framing around window openings, be sure to leave enough margin so you can run your finish material inside the frame opening. Seal between frames and the concrete walls with caulk. Insulate between studs with R-11 or R-19 batt insulation and cover the studs with a 4- or 6-mil polyethylene vapor barrier before installing the wall finish.

Dampness and cold are also problems with a concrete-slab basement floor. If you see evidence of moisture, it's a good idea to treat the entire slab with an epoxy sealer. Be advised, however, that using sealer may prevent you from applying certain types of flooring, such as adhesive-backed vinyl tiles or resilient sheet goods. Refer to the manufacturer's recommendations on the sealer label before you proceed.

Installing a wood-framed floor over a concrete slab solves a number of problems at once. It blocks dampness coming through the slab, levels the floor, and provides a surface that allows you to install a variety of floor surfaces. Remember that installing a new floor "lowers" ceiling height by about 2½ inches.

First install a 6-mil polyethylene vapor barrier over the entire slab. Then place 2×4 pressure-treated studs across the vapor barrier on 24-inch centers. Lay the 2×4s flat, not on their edges, and level them with cedar shims. Nail ¾-inch plywood to the studs at right angles with 1½-inch ring-shank nails. There's no need to fasten the 2×4s to the concrete slab because the plywood will keep them rigid and immobile. Although ceramic tile requires a plywood underlayment of 1¼ inches or more, ¾-inch plywood serves as an underlayment for virtually any other kind of floor surface you wish to install.

■ *In this typical basement (before,* right, *and after,* above*), new walls, windows, and ceiling created a bright and cheery work space. Notice how ducts were rearranged and hidden behind soffits to increase the headroom.*

Light and Heat

If your foundation extends 2 feet or more above ground and is part of the basement, you may be able to install new windows. Because this usually requires cutting concrete or removing cement block, the job is best left to a professional. To gain clearance for a new window, it may be necessary to excavate a window well in the soil outside the window. Window wells admit welcome fresh air and light, but they must be constructed carefully. They are basically open holes and need to be well-drained and covered with a sloping frame of clear, rigid plastic.

Basements are delightfully cool in summer and annoyingly cool in the winter. You can heat them with electric baseboard or space heaters. Because electric heaters draw substantial current and need heavy wiring to work safely, consult a licensed electrician about proper installation.

▲ *Bright wall colors and a delightful trompe l'oeil window banish dreariness from this basement office. It appears the room is facing the courtyard of a sunny country estate in France.*

RADON ALERT

Before you remodel your basement to include a home office, check it for radon—an odorless, colorless gas that occurs naturally in some soils. High levels of radon gas have been identified by the U.S. Surgeon General as a possible cause of lung cancer.

Basements are built below grade, so they are closer to the source of radon gas, which enters through cracks in walls and floors. To test for radon, purchase an inexpensive testing kit at hardware stores or building supply centers. For an accurate reading, perform the test with all basement windows and doors closed; follow the kit directions carefully.

If your results are unacceptably high, consult a qualified contractor who follows radon reduction techniques certified by the U.S. Environmental Protection Agency. The cost for radon abatement measures generally runs from $200 to $3,000, depending on the extent of the work.

For more detailed information, call the Indoor Air Quality Information Clearinghouse, a division of the Environmental Protection Agency, at 800/438-4318. Request the pamphlet #402-K92-003, "Consumer's Guide to Radon Reduction."

Nooks and Crannies

A home office doesn't have to occupy an entire room to be efficient and useful. Many homeowners find their needs adequately addressed by placing a desk, some file storage, and a computer in an out-of-the-way location. Your house probably has several places where an office can be set up without sacrificing living area your family needs for other purposes.

Thanks to the personal computer, which holds a huge amount of information in compact electronic storage, you can create a powerful office with as little as 12 square feet of work surface. Look for locations that can accommodate a built-in desk or work surface customized to fit the available location, and plan to take advantage of all the nearby vertical wall space that you can. The work surface should be at least 54 inches wide and 32 inches deep. You'll also need at least 10 square feet of floor space to allow you to get in and out of your office chair easily and 3 feet of space in front of filing cabinets to allow you to pull out drawers. When planning, don't forget to account for access to electrical power. You may want to install receptacles at desk level so you don't have to route power cords around your work surface or have a tangle of cords at your feet.

Corners of rooms, underneath stairways, and closets are good candidates for conversion to compact home office space. Use the wall space above your desk for shelves that hold supplies and reference materials and the space below it for a filing cabinet. If you want separation between your work area and the rest of the house, use a three-paneled folding screen, a freestanding bookshelf, or large potted plants, all of which make attractive visual barriers.

With careful planning, you may be able to combine a work space with other living areas of your home. For example, a small home office tucked into a corner of the dining room allows you to use the dining room table as an additional work surface during the day. But it will help if

▲ *A now-you-see-it, now-you-don't strategy helps this family room office disappear when not in use.*

► *Hinged cabinet doors on this built-in unit slide out of the way to reveal a computer and bookshelves.*

▲ *Adding a desk surface to a wall of built-in book-shelves and cabinets allows this simple home office* *to neatly blend into the room. The dining table can be borrowed for spreading out projects.*

An efficient work space doesn't have to be big. All you need is a work surface and some storage, as demonstrated by this sleek planning center located in one corner of a dining room.

you're disciplined enough to put away your excess materials each evening and return the shared space to its original use.

If your needs are minimal and a workstation tucked away in a nook or cranny is adequate, you'll probably find a suitable spot for an office. But if space for office equipment and storage is limited, you might have to prioritize your needs. Use the "circle of reach" rule: Place all materials and equipment that are vital to your work needs within easy reach of your office chair. Then find nearby locations for other materials and equipment you need less often.

Here are other suggestions for making the most of a compact office:

☐ Buy a laptop computer instead of a desktop one. Laptops are almost as powerful but occupy a fraction of the desk space. They can be moved easily if you need desk space for other tasks and can be folded up and stored in a drawer.

See Also:
☐ Lighting the Office, pages 64–67
☐ Ergonomics and Health, pages 80-83

☐ Install a wall-mounted telephone.
☐ If you have a desktop computer, place your keyboard on a sliding tray mounted underneath the desk surface.
☐ Use well-placed, small but powerful halogen lamps for task lighting.
☐ If there is a shelf or wall-mounted cabinet over your desk, consider adding strip lights underneath it for task lighting.
☐ Use rolling file cabinets and drawer units that can be stored nearby and pulled out when you need them.
☐ Locate printers or fax machines in other parts of the house. If necessary, consult a licensed electrician about the possibility of having printer cables or telephone wires routed through walls, floors, or ceilings to the desired locations.
☐ Use a wall-mounted bulletin board to keep important messages, business cards, or correspondence in sight but off your desk.

Adding a bank of windows converted this spacious walk-in closet to a light-filled home office. A partition wall constructed to hold clothes reclaims some of the storage lost in the conversion.

▶ *The owners of this home took advantage of unused space beneath the stairs leading to their walk-out basement. Cleverly designed drawers get maximum use from the area and provide office storage.*

Kitchens

Kitchens are increasingly popular locations for home offices. Although there are obvious limitations, such as the size of the work space and the level of professionalism that can be achieved at the hub of your family's activities, a kitchen is usually a warm, friendly place to work. Kitchens make excellent locations for everyday chores, such as clipping coupons, paying bills, writing letters, making shopping lists, and doing homework. Some child development experts endorse the idea that children do better with homework in open family settings than in the relative isolation of their rooms.

If you need to spread out, you can always borrow the kitchen table on a temporary basis. If you have a full-fledged office in another part of your home, you may find that a kitchen-based work space helps keep your professional life separate from household business.

To find space for a kitchen office, you don't necessarily need an expanse of open wall. You can incorporate a desk into a corner, a peninsula or island counter, or a run of lower cabinets. Keep in mind that countertops for lower cabinets have a standard depth of 24 inches and a height of 36 inches. An ideal desk surface should be at least 30 inches deep and no more than 30 inches from the floor. If your kitchen office will include a full-size computer, you'll probably want the desk surface even lower—about 26 inches from the floor—so your screen is at the proper height and the keyboard is at a comfortable level. Look for locations that can accommodate a work surface that is larger and lower than a normal countertop. If none is available, consider having a local cabinetmaker remove an old section of lower cabinets and install a new work surface to your specifications. Computers also require special supplies, so you'll need to find storage for floppy

▲ Kitchen workstations don't have to be camouflaged. This one has a butcher-block work surface that doubles as a food preparation center.

▼ An alcove formed by kitchen cabinets provides the ideal spot for a corner workstation. There's a desk, plenty of storage, and a view to the backyard.

▲ Beautiful cabinets and majestic views command attention here, not the kitchen-based work center neatly tucked into one corner.

◄ A bookshelf unit made in the same style and finish as the kitchen cabinets helps the work center blend into its surroundings.

Kitchens 35

disks and software manuals. If you need a printer or fax machine, consider placing them in a cabinet or large drawer that has been modified to hold equipment and provide access to electrical outlets. Wherever you place your desk, make sure it's out of the way of work areas or other high-traffic locations.

It's a good idea to have your work space blend in with the rest of the kitchen. Cabinet materials, colors, and countertops should complement those throughout the kitchen. Use cabinets and drawers to hide paperwork and supplies and pigeonhole shelves to organize small objects, such as stamps, pads, and staplers. A phone is essential for a kitchen office, but if space is at a premium, install a wall-mounted unit over your desk or at the end of an upper cabinet.

You'll need a strong direct light source. Don't rely on overhead ceiling lights. Use a desk lamp or install lighting under an overhanging upper cabinet that fully illuminates your work surface and helps reduce eyestrain.

▲ *This command center is integral to the kitchen, yet the L-shaped design helps keep it apart from the daily routine of family life, and the raised rail helps prevent accidental misplacing of work materials.*

▶ *The handsome wood cabinetry of this kitchen was extended to create a fully functional office in the center of the home. Tall upper cabinets store materials.*

Master Bedrooms

A master bedroom can make a good location for a home office. It is often large enough to provide room needed for a small but efficient work space, it is usually quiet during the day, and it is often located away from household traffic patterns. There is probably a section of wall you can use to locate a desk, bookshelves, and some filing cabinets without sacrificing personal storage space or essential furniture. If possible, establish your office in a corner location. Corners put storage within easy reach of your desk chair, an especially convenient feature for small offices. A corner desk easily will accommodate a large piece of

▲ *Built-in cabinets provide plenty of storage for a home office that was installed in the dressing room of a master bedroom. A small desk situated in an alcove allows a second work space.*

▶ *Pocket doors leading to a converted dressing room provide privacy for this small bedroom-based office.*

equipment, such as a computer and monitor.

If your master bedroom includes a walk-in closet, you may have an ideal location for a set of bookshelves or a small filing cabinet. If you can provide electrical power to the closet, consider locating electronic equipment such as fax machines or printers there. When you need them, they're only a few steps away. Otherwise, they are neatly out of sight.

One objection to the use of a master bedroom as an office location is the fact that you'll be faced with your work—both night and day. Some people find the idea of introducing fax machines and full wastebaskets into the intimate surroundings of the master bedroom basically intolerable. If you are unable to hide the clutter of your workspace, considering using a three-panel folding screen to create a visual boundary between your work area and the rest of your bedroom.

Because master bedrooms should be primarily restful spaces, give careful consideration to the type of office furnishings you install. The style should harmonize with the existing decor so that the result doesn't detract from the relaxing nature of your bedroom. It is important to preserve the master bedroom's function as one of the more quiet and comfortable environments of your home.

▶ *An office in a renovated walk-in closet keeps this workplace separate from the adjacent master bedroom. To help offset the loss of closet storage, the homeowner used an armoire in the bedroom. Replacing the normal swinging door with a space-saving pocket door allowed room for the armoire to be placed against the bedroom wall.*

▲ *This streamlined bedroom office includes a desk and file storage along one wall, an integrated bookshelf placed on the adjoining wall, and plenty of window light for detailed projects. The style of the work surfaces blends well with the room's decor. The central space is deliberately left open and uncluttered.*

Living, Dining, or Family Rooms

Living, dining, or family rooms can make attractive locations for a home office. Typically, these rooms are large enough to accommodate the needs of a modest home office. There may be interesting architectural features, such as vaulted ceilings, big windows, or a fireplace, that make the space visually intriguing. Also, these rooms are most likely situated on the first level of your home. In that location, they are readily accessible to the outside and provide a comfortable surrounding that is separated from your home's private areas—important features if you plan to meet clients on a regular basis.

Before planning to share an office with a living, dining, or family room, you should carefully evaluate the amount of privacy you think you'll require. These are the main gathering areas for your family, and there may be distractions that interrupt your work. Also, it might be difficult to

➤ *There's plenty of space in this family room for a small corner workstation. Work-related materials are stored in the built-in cabinets.*

THE INSIDE STORY

The spacious family room, *right*, has it all—easy access to the kitchen, plenty of comfortable seating, a great arch-top window, and a home office. Neatly blended into its surroundings, the built-in office cabinetry mimics the woodwork and color of the surrounding moldings and architectural details. Even the workstation chair matches the style of the tall bar chairs at the counter. The open wall space above the desk surface allows the wall color to flow through the office area, further integrating the office within the surrounding family room.

safeguard your valuable papers and projects. If you plan to put an office in a family living area, consider separating it visually from the rest of the room with freestanding bookshelves, a folding screen, or large potted plants. A visual barrier is a great help at establishing boundaries for your office—especially if there are young children in your household.

If you prefer to have your office open to the surrounding room, make sure that office furni-

ture is integrated with your home's decor. Select colors, patterns, or wood tones that blend with the nearby furnishings and wall finishes so the room's original purpose won't be compromised.

Many houses today have an eating area adjacent to the kitchen in addition to a more formal dining room. If so, you may decide that you can do without the dining room altogether and opt to completely convert that space to a home office. This can be an ideal location—comfortable, accessible, and easily made private with swinging or pocket-type doors. The room already will be finished and include lights, windows, and electrical outlets, helping to keep your remodeling costs to a minimum.

See Also:

☐ Nooks and Crannies, pages 30–33

➤ *A now-you-see-it, now-you-don't strategy allows this home office to transform itself into a dining area. During the day, the pine table fits under a wall-hung counter to form an L-shaped workstation. There's access to electricity and a stylish upper kitchen cabinet that provides storage for office supplies or tableware. When needed, the table can be placed in the center of the room for dining and entertaining.*

Garage Conversions

The size of a typical two-car garage is about 500 to 600 square feet. If you're thinking of creating an office in your home, this is a tempting amount of open space. Although a garage conversion is a major remodeling project, the basics are already in place—walls, roof, electricity, and usually a concrete slab floor. The dimensions of the space

◄ *The owner of this house took advantage of his garage space by building over it. Note the separate entrance added to the right of the garage car doors.*

► *The separate entrance provides a convenient covered stairway.*

already should meet codes, so you probably won't have to move walls or raise ceilings. If the garage walls are unfinished, you'll easily be able to run the electrical circuits and telephone wires you need. There already may be an exterior door that can provide a separate entry for your office. If the garage is attached to your home, you'll have access to kitchen and bathroom facilities.

Garage conversion basics

The drawbacks of this kind of conversion are obvious—you'll lose a convenient place to shelter your vehicles, and you'll sacrifice valuable storage for such items as lawn mowers, garden implements, and bicycles. You may be able to compensate with a small backyard garden shed or, if you have a two- or three-car garage, remodel only a portion of the space into a home office. If you choose a partial garage conversion, building codes will likely require the construction of a fire-retardant wall between the garage space and the living area and a fire-retardant ceiling. Drywall at least ⅝-inch thick should provide the necessary com-

THE INSIDE STORY

Although the owner of this over-the-garage conversion originally had established a home office in a spare bedroom, he quickly realized there wasn't enough room for his space-hungry architectural practice. In addition, he received regular visits from clients and needed to create a private office with a professional appearance.

His solution was to remodel the space above his two-car attached garage and build a small addition for an enclosed entrance. For convenience, the new office is linked directly to the house through an upstairs doorway, but the separate entrance keeps traffic out of the main living areas and lends a touch of professionalism to his home-based business.

Big stock windows and white walls fill the interiors with light, while simple track lighting and plain laminate work surfaces helped keep costs down.

▲ *Large windows and soaring ceilings add light and a sense of volume to this over-the-garage conversion.*

◄ *Track lighting lets this home-based architect move task lighting wherever it is needed most.*

pliance. You'll also have to build a floor for your office that is at least 4 inches above any adjacent garage floor. This requirement prevents noxious or flammable vapors from traveling along the floor of the garage and entering a living area.

A garage conversion probably will include insulating the walls and ceiling of your office space, as well as extending your home's heating, ventilation, and cooling (HVAC) systems. Talk to an HVAC expert about placing your garage office on a separate thermostat or, if your home has a programmable thermostat, creating an individual heating and cooling zone for it. Older, single-pane windows should be replaced with units that feature insulating glass. Consider insulating the wall between the garage and your home to help reduce unwanted noise.

The garage door should be replaced with a regular stud wall, as garage doors typically provide very little insulating capabilities and have many air leaks around their edges that make them impractical for living spaces. Remember

▲ *The arrival of a second child prompted the owners of this house to convert their upstairs home office back into a bedroom. To regain their office, they opted to* *remodel this 16×13-foot area over their garage. A shed dormer helped add the necessary headroom, and big skylights provided the daylight.*

that garage doors cannot be used legally as an entrance to a living space, such as an office. Before you begin your remodeling project, it's a good idea to check your local building codes and zoning ordinances about converting a garage to a home office.

A new wall to replace your existing garage doors will be a nonbearing wall because there will already be a load-bearing header in place to take the weight of the joists or rafters. So the new wall will not require a foundation footing underneath it. It can be constructed directly on the concrete slab, but pressure-treated lumber should be used for a bottom plate. A continuous bead of water-proof construction adhesive will ensure a tight, leak-proof bond between the bottom plate and the concrete.

The garage floor is probably a concrete slab that is sloped from back to front to shed water, and on three sides there will be a concrete curb 4 to 6 inches high. Most garage slabs are in direct contact with the soils below, which means that in winter the slab tends to stay cool and absorb heat from any nearby radiant sources, such as your feet and lower legs. In cooler weather, sitting in a chair with your feet on a concrete slab will make your feet and legs feel chilly even though the rest of your body is comfortable.

The remedy for both the slope and the cold is to construct a level wood-frame floor over the existing slab. First, cover the slab with a 6-mil polyethylene vapor barrier. Then install framing lumber—pressure-treated wood studs placed flat—on 16-inch centers. Level the framing lumber with wooden shims, and then fill the cavities between the studs with pieces cut from 1-inch rigid foam insulation board. Cover the framing members with ¾-inch plywood.

For more insulating capabilities or to provide the space for heating ducts, place the framing grid on edge and fill the cavities with fiberglass batt insulation. Either method will raise the level of

▶ *The enclosed stairway in the corner of this garage leads up from the adjoining dining room to an office above the garage. The solution didn't rob the garage of storage or parking space—the car slips beneath the slanted stairway.*

the floor, so be sure to check your headroom requirements before you begin.

An office over the garage

Another potential home office space is in the area above the garage. This area is basically an attic space, and the evaluation and conversion of it will follow the same guidelines as presented on pages 20–25. If you convert this space, building codes likely will require that you install material such as ⅝-inch drywall to create a fire-retardant ceiling for the parking area below your office.

One advantage of creating an office over your garage is that it will be relatively simple to construct a private entrance on the outside of the garage. Visitors to your home office will appreciate having an entrance that doesn't intrude on your home's living areas. If you do construct a private entrance, make sure your addition complies with any setback regulations established by your community.

See Also:

☐ Zoning Ordinances and Restrictions, page 10
☐ Attics, pages 20–25

Kids' Rooms

Homework will seem less of a chore for children who have a comfortable, well-organized place to study, read, draw, or work on the computer. Kids' workstations should have many of the same conveniences and features of any adult-size office—plenty of storage, an adequate work surface, good lighting, and an ergonomically designed chair—only on a smaller scale.

It's important that children have easy access to everything they'll need, so plan for low bookshelves and cabinets that don't require an awkward reach. You don't want your child hauling out a chair to stand on to reach the top of a bookshelf. Desks and other work surfaces should be no more than 24 inches from front to back so kids can reach across them easily. Computer workstations may need to be 30 inches or more deep to accommodate monitors, so consider installing a corner desk unit or providing a separate work table for the computer.

Drawers and cabinets with doors help keep cluttered shelves out of sight, and it's a good idea to provide oversized storage, such as a cabinet with double doors, for safekeeping of projects-in-progress. Desk organizers that hold small items, such as pens and pencils, are a must.

Whether you decide to purchase furniture from a retail outlet or catalog, or design your own built-ins, you'll want to plan for growth. Many child-size desks, tables, and chairs are adjustable so they can be raised as your child grows. If you are making built-ins, plan work surfaces that are adjustable. A simple laminate-covered desk surface resting on adjustable, wall-mounted guides will keep the work area ergonomically correct for many years.

▲ *Playful sleeping cubicles are mated to the nearby work area with colorful matching laminate surfaces. Carpet cut in a free-flowing pattern mimics the furniture's hues. Storage extends around the base of the sleeping cubicles and is readily accessible to children of any age.*

▶ *Kids love small places designed with their special needs in mind. This desk alcove was designed for a corner of a child's room in a newly built house. There's plenty of windows for light and fresh air, and the soffit makes an ideal location for recessed lighting. A small table nearby holds ongoing projects and is a great place to play board games.*

ERGONOMICS FOR CHILDREN

Age in years	1–4	5–7	8–10	11–14
Chair seat height	12"	12–14"	13–17"	15–18"
Table height	18"	20–24"	24–27"	26–30"

Kids' Rooms

If possible, provide undercounter lighting for your child's work surface. Be cautious when considering desk lamps with halogen bulbs. Halogen bulbs burn at extremely high temperatures that can ignite papers or cloth if accidentally knocked over. Consider desk lamps with fluorescent bulbs that burn at relatively cool temperatures.

Children's rooms and work areas should be fun and cheerful spaces, but select workplace furnishings that won't seem too babyish in a few years. You always can change wallpapers or paint colors, but consider desks and chairs that won't go out of style as your child matures.

▶ *Photos of real Dalmations were used to re-create the big black spots that adorn this fun-filled kids' study area. A stock laminate desk provides plenty of drawer storage, and the big shelf over the desk features strip lighting underneath. The window seat makes a cozy and inviting place to read.*

▲ *Creating a quiet place to do homework was the primary goal of a remodeling project that converted a hallway and large closet into this dedicated study area. Corner desks make good locations for computer workstations.*

Additions

Adding on to your home may be the ideal way to create an office within your home. If you build an addition, you'll be able to design an office that accommodates your needs and is an expression of your personal style. Building an addition is also one of the more expensive options for creating a home office, so careful planning and budgeting will be essential to the success of the project.

Before you begin, you should determine if your planned remodeling is a good value. To help you decide, you should be familiar with the average real estate values of other homes in your neighborhood. If the current market value of your home plus the cost of an new addition would exceed average prices of similar homes in your area by more than 15 percent, you may be too ambitious. A fabulous addition might provide great living area, but if you decide to sell your home, you may not be able to recover the cost of your investment. Talk to local real estate professionals to get estimates of prices of the houses in your area.

Because additions are complex projects, it's a good idea to engage the services of an architect or reliable design/build team. These professionals should be able to anticipate problems, provide construction drawings that meet all building

▼ *A grand remodeling of this 1860 farmhouse included the addition of a new garage and a 575-square-foot second-story office over the garage space. Dramatic window groupings in each gable add architectural interest, and clapboard siding unifies the new portions of the house with the old.*

▶ This customized space meets every need of the owner, a home-based architect. There are lots of windows for daylight, built-in storage, wide work surfaces, and a conference area for meeting with clients.

codes, and give reliable estimates of the total cost. If you prefer, you can hire a design professional for consultation work only, and keep their involvement to a minimum. If you act as your own architect or general contractor, your project still must meet all codes and be open to periodic visits from the local building inspector. You also must obtain a construction permit from your zoning and planning commission.

An office addition does not necessarily mean building a whole new room. A small bump-out, if well-planned, could provide the space for a desk and enough shelves and storage to meet your needs. Although bump-outs are more modest remodeling projects, they can have many of the same requirements as larger additions—footings and a foundation, a roof, insulated walls, electrical circuits, and construction drawings that have been approved by a registered structural engineer or architect.

Even a modest remodeling will have an effect on your normal routine. Your home will be open to dust, construction noise, and a work crew. Electrical and plumbing services may be interrupted for periods, and you may find you need to leave your home from time to time to escape the inevitable mess. Hopefully, the results will justify any inconveniences you must endure.

See Also:

☐ Understanding Building Codes, pages 58–59
☐ You As General Contractor, page 59

Separate Structures

If you have enough space on your property and your local zoning laws will allow it, you might want to build a small structure to serve as your home office. You'll have complete separation from your main living quarters, privacy, and the opportunity to customize the office to suit your needs—yet everything will be only a few steps away from your home. While it's a good idea to have the architectural style be in harmony with your main house, it's also a rare opportunity for a flight of fancy. You might enjoy the idea of working in a whimsical European cottage, miniature barn, or Japanese pagoda.

This is also the most expensive option for establishing a home-based office. Expect to pay $75 to $130 per square foot for new construction. Whatever utilities you require—water, natural gas, or electricity—must be brought to the structure, as well as telephone lines and, if desired, a communication link to your home such as an intercom system. Extending these services from your home to the new office will add to the cost of construction. You also might need heat, air-conditioning, fully insulated walls and ceiling, and possibly a toilet. In short, this type of home office is really a small house, complete with its own systems, and will benefit from as much careful planning as you can provide.

Zoning and Utilities

Your first step should be a visit to your planning and zoning commission to check if it's feasible to build a separate home office on your property. Most municipalities place restrictions on the kind of outbuildings that can be constructed in residential neighborhoods, and outbuildings that include utilities, such as electricity and plumbing, are the most tightly regulated. Be sure to check for options that will allow you to comply with

▲ *Built-in cabinets and shelves make this stand-alone home office an efficient and well-organized work environment. Windows offer plenty of light and provide cross-ventilation during the warmer months.*

▶ *The owner of this separate home office enjoys country living so much that he created his work space to look like a barn. Wide steps welcome visitors and clients.*

zoning regulations. For example, you may be able to construct a home office if you provide only electricity and abandon your plans for plumbing. Be aware of any other restrictions, such as setback laws that regulate how close you are allowed to build to your lot line or ordinances that govern the height of your new structure.

To run electrical or telecommunications services to your new office location, your best option is to place them underground to avoid having wires or utility poles cluttering up your yard. Underground services require a narrow trench at least 18 inches deep to be dug from the point of origin (your house) to the office. Take the opportunity to run your telephone lines in the same trench; but telephone lines should be protected by metal or plastic conduit.

Your new electrical service will branch off your home's main panel. If you want to provide more than one circuit for your office, you'll have to have a branch panel installed on the new outbuilding. It's a good idea to hire an electrical contractor to do this type of wiring.

Plumbing must be placed in the ground below the frost line to prevent lines from freezing. In northern climates this may be as much as 36 inches below the surface. The plumbing lines should be insulated fully at the location where they emerge from the ground and enter the office —a particularly important point if your office is built on a raised foundation that includes a crawl space. Structures with plumbing also must be heated continually throughout the year to pre-

▲ *Nestled at the back of a half-acre lot, this stand-alone home office enjoys peaceful, quiet surroundings and is only a short walk from the main house.*

vent pipes from freezing. If you leave for an extended period you may turn your heat down but not off.

While bringing utilities to a separate structure is one matter, providing the waste pipes needed for a toilet and lavatory is quite another. Waste pipes require a continuous downward pitch or "fall" from the toilet to a sewer line or septic tank. Determining if your property can provide adequate fall will require the expert advice of a

plumbing professional. Otherwise, consider installing a portable toilet that has the ability to disinfect waste.

Understanding Building Codes

Building codes can be confusing and exasperating, but they're a fact of life for anyone planning a sizeable project, such as a separate structure or a major home remodeling project. If you build or remodel without the proper government permits, you could face fines and the loss of your house insurance coverage.

On the positive side, obtaining a building permit adds to your safety. Codes set minimum acceptable standards for structural integrity, sanitation system design, proper ventilation, adequate natural light, and electrical circuits. The process ensures that your contractor's work will be checked periodically by an unbiased third party—a building inspector—who will examine all work for compliance with safety regulations and guidelines.

To reduce their financial losses, insurance companies helped develop and promote the National Building Code. Most jurisdictions base their local codes upon the National Building Code, the Uniform Building Code, or the Standard Building Code. The Council of American Building Officials (CABO) studies and works with these building codes to consolidate and simplify them, and the CABO set of codes generally is recognized as the most thoughtful and clearly presented.

Once adopted, codes are typically revised every three years. To avoid violations, contractors must keep up with pertinent revisions. Recent changes to building codes have emphasized safety and energy efficiency. Some jurisdictions require windows to be insulated and as efficient as triple-pane units. For new construction, most codes now require smoke alarms that are permanently wired—not battery-operated units.

Code requirements may vary by locale, but there are many common elements.
☐ Typically, the size of bedroom windows can be no less than 8 percent of the floor area. Half the windows must open, and at least one must provide an emergency exit in case of fire.
☐ Bedrooms must contain no less than 70 square

◄ Fourteen-foot-tall ceilings and an exposed truss give this stand-alone home office architectural interest. The high ceilings prevent the space from feeling cramped.

☐ Ceilings must be at least 7 feet, 6 inches high, with no beams projecting down more than 6 inches. This is an important factor in basement and attic remodeling projects.

☐ New furnaces that are not sealed-combustion units must have outside air supplied through ductwork.

☐ Some building codes insist that a toilet be at least 30 inches from the center of the drain to the adjacent walls. This factor can be an especially important consideration for small bathrooms that service home offices.

◄ This 12×16-foot stand-alone home office has a built-in workstation, comfortable furnishings to accommodate guests, and a private bathroom.

feet of floor area, with 7 feet being the shortest wall dimension allowed.

☐ Any stairway with three steps or more must have a railing 30 to 34 inches above the tread. Codes usually specify steps with an 11-inch deep "run" or horizontal surface, and a 7½-inch "rise" or vertical surface.

You as General Contractor

If you act as your own general contractor you will be responsible for compliance with all building codes. In this regard a good relationship with your building inspector can be invaluable. On occasion, your building inspector may be able to stop by and offer advice on the correct procedures or methods for code compliance so that your work will be able to pass an official inspection. If you hire a general contractor, that person will be responsible for obtaining all permits and making sure the work passes inspections. Be sure that your contract with a general contractor specifically requires the contractor and all subcontractors to meet or exceed all applicable building codes.

New Homes

If you're planning to build a new home, you have an excellent opportunity to plan a home office ideally suited to your needs. Carefully evaluate how much privacy you need and whether or not your office must be accessible to visits from clients.

An architect or qualified design professional can help you create an ideal home office. It may be as simple as renaming a room from an existing home plan—turning the first-floor bedroom into an office, for example—or you may want a more customized solution that defines your office with a unique shape and location. On paper, anything is possible, but out-of-the-ordinary requests will certainly require extra time during the building process and more money from you. Ask your architect to keep you apprised of any additional costs a customized office might add to the total cost of building your house.

A home office you plan from the beginning can be almost any size. An office for one full-time occupant can be established in a 10×12-foot area, and anything larger can provide room for built-in cabinets and additional work surfaces or simply add a sense of spaciousness. An office for two occupants should be at least 12×17 feet and offer sensible separation of materials, files, equipment, and personal items.

When designing a home office from scratch, here are some ideas to keep in mind:

☐ Place offices on the first level for accessibility, on the second level for privacy. A second-level office should include normal closet space so that it can be converted easily to bedroom use by future owners.

☐ For privacy, place the office so that it is accessible only through a "private corridor," such as the master bedroom.

◀ *Located above the front entry of this newly built two-story home, a lofty office features windows on three sides and excellent views. The location also isolates the office from everyday household noises.*

THE INSIDE STORY

Built to take advantage of a narrow, wooded lot, this two-story Minneapolis home features plenty of glass that offers views of the surrounding trees and property. Positioning the second-level office over the entryway separates it from other upstairs living areas, and the bump-out design affords a unique feature—the office has windows on three sides. Two-story-high open interior areas flank the entry to the office, creating a short bridge from the upstairs hallway to the entry door of the office. The unique configuration gives the 12×10-foot work space plenty of quiet, privacy, and, according to the homeowner, "an almost tree-house quality."

▲ *Wrap-around work surfaces provide space to spread out projects and reference materials. The windows of this office face three different directions and gather lots of ambient daylight.*

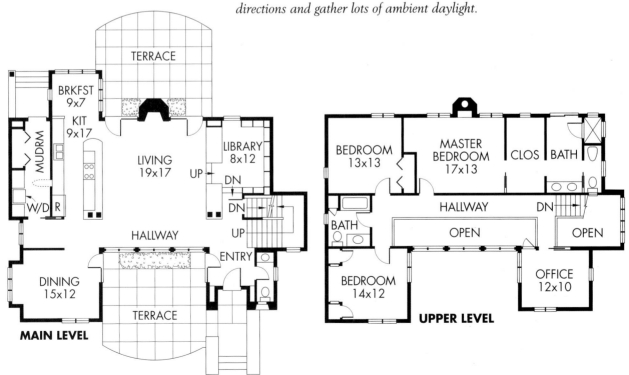

MAIN LEVEL

TERRACE

BRKFST 9x7

KIT 9x17

MUDRM

W/D R

LIVING 19x17

LIBRARY 8x12

UP

DN

DN

UP

HALLWAY

ENTRY

DINING 15x12

TERRACE

UPPER LEVEL

BEDROOM 13x13

MASTER BEDROOM 17x13

CLOS

BATH

BATH

HALLWAY

DN

OPEN

OPEN

BEDROOM 14x12

OFFICE 12x10

□ Try to anticipate your needs both now and in the future, and have your office wired accordingly. You may want the office placed on its own electrical circuit, and you may need more than one telephone line. Wiring now, while walls are open, is a lot less expensive and troublesome than any time after the house is finished completely. If you enjoy music, don't forget to have speaker wires placed in the walls, too.

□ For excellent sound insulation, have the floor, ceiling, and all walls filled with fiberglass batts. Install a solid-core door instead of a hollow-core one. Remember that extra insulation may keep your office quiet, but it also will be insulated from the rest of the house thermally. You should place your office on its own thermostat to effectively regulate the temperature.

▲ *Built in 1989, this suburban house featured a conventional floor plan with a master bedroom suite located on the first floor. It was a simple matter to designate the master bedroom as a spacious office featuring a private bathroom and a generous storage area situated in the walk-in closet.*

See Also:

▶ *Elegant wallpaper and warm-toned antiques create a soothing color palette for this master bedroom converted to an office for a corporate employee who works full time at home.*

▼ *An antique armoire makes handsome hideaway storage for office supplies.*

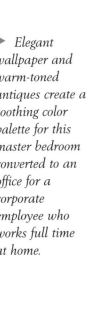

□ Consider adding an indirect lighting scheme that can be hidden in moldings or other architectural features. Indirect lighting is bounced off the ceiling for a soft, ambient light that is ideal for keeping glare off computer monitors.

□ Now is the time to consider any built-in cabinets or shelves. If possible, work with your architect to establish a satisfactory design for any cabinetry. Or, work with a qualified designer from a custom cabinet shop or kitchen design center. Many of today's kitchen cabinet manufacturers feature a full line of cabinets and shelving intended for all areas of the home.

Practical Matters

Make sure all systems are in place before you finish and furnish your home office.

Once you've established a space for a home office, you'll want to make sure that space is as efficient and hardworking as possible. This means that essential needs—lighting, electrical power, telecommunications requirements, and sound insulation—have all been accounted for before you add furnishings and supplies.

Lighting the Office

Proper lighting helps make the home office environment efficient, comfortable, and productive. Improper lighting can shorten the hours you're able to work and produce many of the chronic symptoms of eye fatigue—itching eyes, blurred vision, backaches, and headaches. No office plan is complete without a plan for proper lighting.

Today's office environment is complicated by the computer monitor, which requires low light levels for viewing but must coexist with regular paperwork, which needs higher light levels. The computer monitor should face away from or be at right angles to windows so that glare is avoided.

There are two basic types of lighting—ambient and task. Ambient lighting is general lighting that fills the entire work space. It is soft and diffuse and can be produced by several sources at once. Task lighting is light directed onto a specific work area and usually is created by a single lighting source.

Daylight provides lots of natural, cheerful, ambient light, and broad expanses of glass, unusual-shaped windows, or excellent views can be one of the great benefits of the home-based office. But designing an office to avoid direct sunlight and window glare can be tricky. As a rule of thumb, never have a window directly behind a computer screen. The resulting glare can cause serious eyestrain. Also, it is not a good idea to place a monitor so that you're looking directly at a window while working on your computer. The difference in the intensity of the light values—those of your monitor and that produced by the window

▶ *This well-appointed home office demonstrates the benefits of good planning. Window glare is controlled by shutter-type blinds, and a table lamp provides task lighting. The computer screen faces away from the window to avoid glare.*

directly behind it—can contribute to eye fatigue. The best solution is to place the computer monitor at right angles to sources of window light. Create flexibility with blinds or shades that can be adjusted for different light conditions. Blinds have the advantage of being able to redirect sunlight upward, where it can be reflected off a ceiling as soft, ambient light.

For working at night or on cloudy days, you'll need an artificial source of ambient light. The room where you work may include an overhead light, but check to make sure this light is not reflected in your computer monitor. You may want to connect an overhead light source to a rheostat switch that will allow you to control the intensity of the light. The best sources of ambient light are those that direct the light toward the ceiling but don't cause glare. Floor lamps, table lamps, or wall sconces with dark shades are good sources of this type of lighting, or you might consider installing an indirect lighting scheme that is camouflaged behind architectural moldings.

Task lighting directs light onto a specific area for reading or writing. Undercounter lights placed beneath a shelf situated over your desk can provide good task lighting, but you won't be able to vary the intensity of the light. Desk lamps that have flexible arms and moveable heads can be placed on the work surface to provide adjustable task lighting. Adjustable task lighting helps avoid the glare that white paper or coated magazine pages can produce. The standard for proper lighting of reading materials is about 80 footcandles of light intensity, which can be produced by a single 60-watt bulb in a standard desk lamp at a distance of 12 to 18 inches from your work. Don't rely on ceiling-mounted fixtures for task lighting. The resulting light is usually too harsh—creating glare and shadows throughout the workplace.

Producing both ambient light for working at the computer and task lighting for reading research materials at the same time can be tricky. Moving your eyes back and forth between the two can cause eyestrain and headaches. The solution is to have a task lighting source that is

▼ *A sleek, ergonomically designed lamp provides task lighting. The design permits the base to be located away from the illuminated surface, allowing plenty of space for work materials. (From Waldmann Lighting.)*

relatively small and easily maneuvered so that you can adequately light your reading materials without producing a glare on your monitor.

Electrical Requirements

Today's home office can be a technological marvel. Fax machines, personal copiers, computers, laser printers, modems, and sophisticated answering machines are only a few of the many electronic devices that increasingly influence the ability to work at home. To keep your office running smoothly—and safely—you should anticipate the electrical power requirements for your office, and keep in mind any future expansion or additional equipment you might need.

Most rooms are already wired to handle a moderate electrical load, and office equipment will not by itself tax the system excessively. What may occur, however, is that the circuit that services your office also services other areas of your home. It could mean that if someone is vacuuming the downstairs hallway and you turn on your laser printer, a circuit breaker will trip, interrupting your work and jeopardizing information currently on your computer screen.

For convenience and safety, it's a good idea to isolate your office on its own circuit. Any electrical space heaters or window-type air-conditioners in your office also should be placed on their own electrical circuits. A licensed electrician will be able to map your home's electrical supply and devise a way to provide your office with the circuits required.

Most household circuits are rated for either 15 or 20 amps, which you can check at your main circuit breaker panel. If the circuits in your panel are not marked, you can find which circuit feeds your office by trial and error. Switch breakers on and off until you discover which circuit supplies your office, then check the breaker itself for its amp rating. To give you an idea of the load requirements of typical office equipment, refer to the summary in the table on page 68. Each piece of electrical equipment you have should have an amp rating on its Underwriters Laboratories (UL) tag or on its packaging material.

You'll want to make sure outlets are conveniently located. Building codes require that no space along a wall be more than 6 feet from an

▲ *Task lighting is produced by a single light source and illuminates a specific area. Undercabinet and desktop fixtures produce task lighting.*

▲ *Ambient light is general room lighting produced by many sources. Daylight from windows and light that reflects off walls and ceilings are types of ambient light.*

outlet. Roughly translated, it means there probably should be one or two outlets available on every wall of living area in your home. The number of plugs those outlets can handle, however, may be woefully inadequate for the many devices you need. In addition to office equipment, there may be desk lamps, stereos, televisions, and coffeemakers. Also, electrical plugs tend to cluster around a single outlet, creating the infamous "octopus" tangle of cords and wires that is an unattractive by-product of modern technology.

The solution is to install more outlets, evenly distributed around the room. The National Electrical Code advises no more than nine outlets on a 15-amp circuit or a maximum of 12 outlets for a 20-amp circuit. To help visualize how many outlets you'll need, sketch out your planned office and where equipment will be located. If you know for certain that most of your equipment will be grouped near one wall, make sure that wall has plenty of outlets.

Device	Amps
Computer	2.5–3
Monitor	1.5–2.5
Laser printer	6–7
Ink jet printer	1
Fax machine	1.5
Desk lamp	0.5
Coffeemaker	7–8
Portable heater	13

You can increase the capacity of a single outlet with a multioutlet surge suppressor that provides space for an additional six or eight plugs. These devices sense surges in current that might be harmful to sensitive machinery and instantaneously interrupt the flow of current. Invest in good quality surge suppressors guaranteed to prevent damage to your system. Be aware that common surge suppressors may not be able to protect your equipment if lightning strikes your home, even if your home has a properly grounded lightning rod. You can purchase surge suppressors that are warranted to protect against the violent surges in electrical current caused by lightning strikes, but be prepared to pay a premium price for these devices.

▶ *Surge suppressors, top, and uninterrupted power supply (UPS) units, bottom, protect sensitive electronic equipment from fluctuations in electrical current. (From APC.)*

If uninterrupted power is vital to you or your business, you may want to consider an uninterrupted power supply (UPS) with a line conditioner. A UPS is a plug-in device that protects equipment in two ways. First, it provides supplemental battery power in the event of a power outage. The supplemental power can last 15 minutes, long enough to save valuable data and shut down equipment. Secondly, a UPS provides an even, regulated power supply. Because the power that flows to your home is constantly undergoing minor fluctuations, the "conditioning" capability of a UPS can help reduce electronic wear and tear and increase the life span of your sensitive equipment.

Communications

Today's home office can be a communications powerhouse featuring telephones, answering machines, fax machines, and modem connections to the information superhighway. The proliferation of the home office is due in large part to the variety of tasks these pieces of equipment enable us to accomplish. While these machines are a great benefit for the home-based worker, they all compete for use of your telephone lines and for space inside your office. To accommodate these devices, you should carefully plan where they will be located and where telephone wires will run. In addition to your regular home phone line, you'll need another line or two exclusively for your business. This keeps your home line free for casual use and prevents personal calls from interrupting business communications.

No matter how many telecommunications devices or lines you have, flexibility is the key to

▲ This "octopus" of electrical wires, printer cables, and telephone lines is an unfortunate—and unsightly—product of today's technology.

▶ It's difficult to remove an octopus, but it can be effectively camouflaged with furniture and plants.

planning. You should have two or three telephone jacks installed around the room that will permit you to shift furnishings and move telecommunications devices wherever you need. Each jack should provide a plug for your private home line as well as your business lines. For example, if you're bound to your desk but need to be on the alert for an important call coming on your home line, you can simply plug in a telephone on a temporary basis.

Telecommunications companies offer a variety of services of benefit to the home-based worker. To see what kind of services—and prices—these companies provide, contact a sales representative. Services of interest to the home office include:

☐ Call waiting. An intermittent tone sounds in your ear if you are on the phone and another call is coming in. A touch of your phone's hang-up button will switch you back and forth between callers.

☐ Caller identification. A small screen displays the number of the party who is currently calling, allowing you to decide whether to accept the call. Sophisticated devices also will place the phone numbers of recent callers in retrievable memory.

☐ Distinctive ring. A single line carries two phone numbers that are distinguished by the type of ringing tones they produce.

☐ Internet service. Many companies now provide access to the World Wide Web for a monthly fee.

☐ Call forwarding. For a nominal fee, you can have incoming calls transferred to an answering service if your line is busy.

☐ Convenience billing. For a nominal fee, some service providers can group your long-distance calls according to three-digit codes that you enter for each call. When your monthly bill arrives, your calls are already sorted by account. This can be a helpful service if you make many calls on behalf of clients and need to bill the clients for the amounts.

Insulating Against Noise

When it comes to your home office, the sweetest sound you hear might be the sound of silence. Ringing phones, televisions, and giggling teenagers are all part of the general hubbub of daily life, but if you are a home-based contractor trying to make a deadline, the unwanted noise can disrupt your concentration and even jeopardize your production. Some people are unaffected by noises; others impose strict family noise-abatement guidelines; and others may choose to create an office environment that protects against unwanted noise with sound-dampening materials and strategies.

Unwanted noise comes in two types—sounds that enter the work space from another part of your house or from the outdoors and ambient

▲ Curtains and material draped in front of hard wall surfaces can help reduce ambient noise within the office by absorbing sound.

▶ Hard surface flooring, such as wood or tile, is beautiful but can produce harsh footfalls. Help reduce noises with throw rugs.

noise generated inside your office. If you are sensitive to noise, you probably will want to create an office designed to reduce both types.

Noise can enter a room in much the same manner as air—through cracks and openings—and it's a good idea to provide your office with a tight-fitting door that will help eliminate unwanted noise. Install a threshold and fit the bottom of your door with a weatherproof sweep to prevent noise from entering underneath the door. Add weather stripping to the door jamb. You might also consider replacing your hollow-core interior passage door with a solid door. Solid

doors are much more effective at blocking noise that lighter, hollow-core doors. Solid doors may require that a third hinge be attached to your door jamb to support the extra weight.

Probably the most prevalent unwanted noise, besides televisions and stereos, is footfalls. This is especially true if a basement or first-level office has a well-used room directly above it. Installing a carpet and pad in adjacent rooms can cut sound levels almost 40 percent. If you have access to joist or stud spaces, as might be the case if you are remodeling or converting an attic or basement to an office, take the opportunity to fill the cavities with fiberglass insulation. An insulated 3½-inch stud wall can reduce noise transmitted through it by more than 50 percent, and 6 inches of insulation between floor or ceiling joists reduce noise even more.

If you don't have access to the insides of walls, ceilings, or floors, you can add sound-deadening materials to existing surfaces that will help reduce noise transmission. Acoustic tile ceilings, also known as suspended ceilings, can create an effective sound barrier and are relatively inexpensive to install. In basements, suspended ceilings have the added advantage of being able to hide pipes and wires while still permitting service access to systems.

Acoustic plaster, which is plaster mixed with lightweight vermiculite compounds, can be applied directly to drywall surfaces. Also available are fiber-based sound-deadening compounds that are sprayed on with special equipment. If possible, leave the finish surfaces of these materials rough. The texture will help reduce reflected sounds. Acoustic plasters or compounds can be applied to both sides of a wall if you want maximum sound-deadening effect, but you will have to account for any increase in wall thickness at doors and windows by adding jamb extensions and at electrical outlets by moving electrical boxes or installing retrofit boxes.

Another effective but more expensive way to reduce sound transmission is to screw another layer of drywall to resilient metal channels. Resilient channels help reduce noise transmission by flexing slightly to absorb vibrations. Resilient channels usually are installed at right angles to joists and studs and are designed to be used for

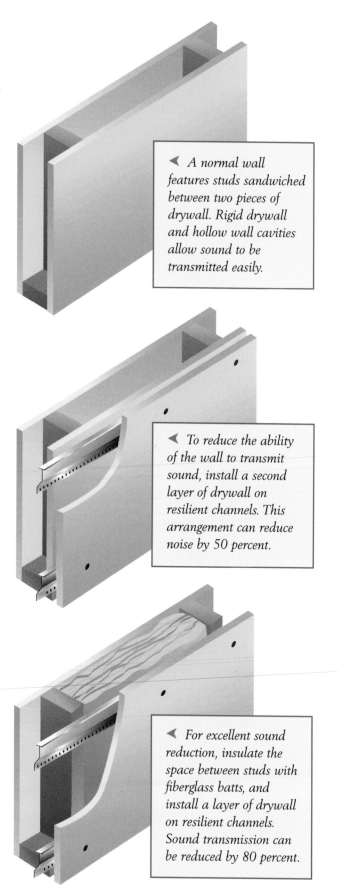

◄ A normal wall features studs sandwiched between two pieces of drywall. Rigid drywall and hollow wall cavities allow sound to be transmitted easily.

◄ To reduce the ability of the wall to transmit sound, install a second layer of drywall on resilient channels. This arrangement can reduce noise by 50 percent.

◄ For excellent sound reduction, insulate the space between studs with fiberglass batts, and install a layer of drywall on resilient channels. Sound transmission can be reduced by 80 percent.

walls, floors, or ceilings. For more sound deadening, use ⅝-inch drywall instead of conventional ½-inch stock. As mentioned above, adding thickness to walls must be accounted for at doors and windows by adding jamb extensions and at electrical outlets by moving electrical boxes or installing retrofit boxes.

There is little you can do to reduce street noise other than move your office to a side of your home that faces away from roads and traffic. If that's not possible, then make sure your window glass is double- or triple-pane, and cover your windows with heavy drapes.

Ambient noise comes from many sources—humming computers, noisy keyboards, and raspy furnace motors. One of the best ways to reduce unwanted ambient noise is by using plenty of soft, sound-absorbing materials when it comes to finishing and furnishing your office. Carpets are helpful in eliminating noise in both directions—the noise you generate inside your office as you walk around and noise that occurs below your office as a result. For sound deadening purposes, the thicker the better, and don't forget the carpet pads. You might want to install carpets in nearby areas as well, such as hallways or adjacent rooms. If your office has wood or tile floors, you can soften footfalls with throw rugs.

Window drapes and even overstuffed furniture will help absorb and reduce ambient noise in your office. Wall hangings, such as tapestries or woven art, can be used in place of framed artwork to prevent glass from reflecting sound.

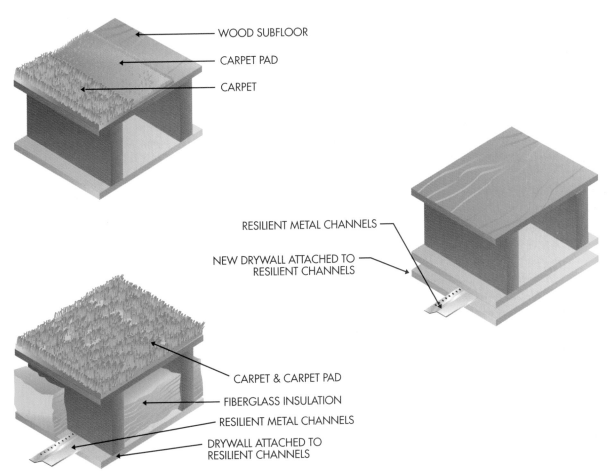

WOOD SUBFLOOR
CARPET PAD
CARPET

RESILIENT METAL CHANNELS
NEW DRYWALL ATTACHED TO RESILIENT CHANNELS

CARPET & CARPET PAD
FIBERGLASS INSULATION
RESILIENT METAL CHANNELS
DRYWALL ATTACHED TO RESILIENT CHANNELS

▲ *Insulate floors against sound transmission by installing carpets and pads. A medium-pile carpet and foam pad (top) will reduce noise 40 percent. A second layer of drywall screwed to resilient channels (middle) will also reduce transmission by 40 percent. Reduce noise passing through floors by 90 percent with a combination of carpet, pad, drywall attached to resilient channels, and fiberglass insulation (bottom).*

Designing Your Office

Make your office a productive and creative environment through sensible design and comfortable furnishings.

An L-shaped desk and built-in bookshelves keep essential items— computer, telephone, and reference books— close at hand, yet provide plenty of open work space for projects in progress.

There are no exact rules for good office design, but some common-sense guidelines can make your office an efficient and inviting work space. No matter how you configure your office, you'll need to organize your materials and equipment for convenience by establishing three zones. The first zone is your immediate work area and contains essential materials arranged so they can be reached easily. If you make frequent use of an appointment calendar, sales catalogs, or your telephone, place these items in drawers or on shelves not more than an arm's length away from your office chair. If you consult many reference books each day, position a bookshelf close to your workstation. Your immediate work area should include an open desk or table surface so current projects are close at hand.

Items that must be readily accessible, but are not needed every day, can be placed in a second zone a few steps from your desk. Put them on bookshelves and in filing cabinets around the perimeter of your office. This is also a good place for office equipment, such as fax machines and printers. If possible, route electrical cords and cables so you can locate office equipment away from your immediate work area.

If having enough office space is a concern, consider establishing a third zone for nonessential items. For example, your last five years of tax records or extra paper for your printer could be stored anywhere in your house. Place items you need infrequently outside your office environment to maximize space.

Organize your office according to how often you'll need various items. Place essentials within an arm's reach—a primary zone no more than 28 to 30 inches away. Include your vertical reach and the areas at your sides and behind you. Items that aren't used every day should be kept out of this zone.

Creating a Layout

Start by working out possible solutions on paper. This allows you to arrange furniture, storage, and telecommunications and other equipment and make sensible traffic patterns. Once you've made a sound preliminary design on paper, you can plan electrical outlets, telephone jacks, and built-in cabinets.

First, consider the primary function of your office. If you use a computer or drafting table every day, its location should have top priority. If you expect clients, providing comfortable seating or a small conference table is essential. Once you have established priorities, you can build an efficient and aesthetically pleasing layout.

Make an Outline Drawing

Make an outline of your office using the grid paper on page 79. Include the dimensions of any closets. Sketch in all doors and include the arc of the door swing. Interior doors typically swing into rooms, so allowing for the arc of the swing becomes critical for positioning furniture. Show all window locations and indicate the location of all existing electrical outlets and telephone jacks.

Once the basic outline is completed, make photocopies of the furniture outlines and symbols on page 78, or create others to your needs at a scale of ½ inch equals 1 foot. Use cutouts of the furniture outlines to experiment with different arrangements. Add new electrical outlets and telephone jacks where needed. If you have artwork or wall hangings you'd like to use, now is the time to consider where they fit best.

Work-Space Configurations

No matter what the size or shape of the room you'll use for an office, the arrangement of your first-zone work space likely will be one of five basic configurations, *far right*. Start with one of these basic shapes, then add shelves, file cabinets, and furniture for the second zone.

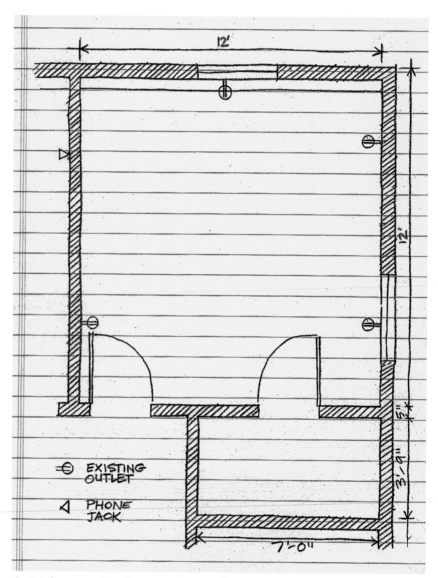

▲ *Make an outline drawing of your office space to help plan the placement of furniture, storage, and equipment. To make the drawing accurate and to scale, photocopy the graph paper on page 79. Your drawing should include windows, doors, closets, electrical outlets, and telephone jacks.*

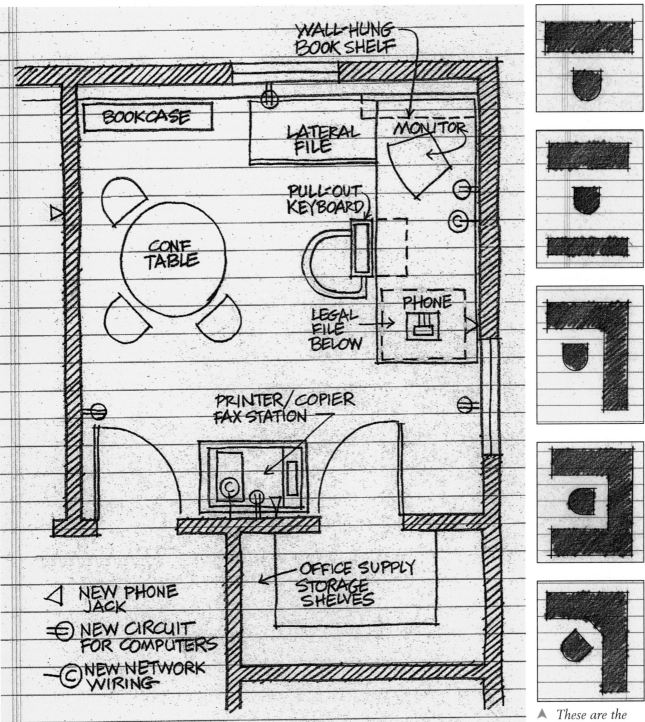

WALL-HUNG
BOOK SHELF

BOOKCASE

LATERAL
FILE

MONITOR

PULL-OUT
KEYBOARD

CONF
TABLE

LEGAL
FILE
BELOW

PHONE

PRINTER/COPIER
FAX STATION

◁ NEW PHONE
JACK

⊖ NEW CIRCUIT
FOR COMPUTERS

© NEW NETWORK
WIRING

OFFICE SUPPLY
STORAGE
SHELVES

▲ Experiment with the placement of furnishings, storage, and equipment on your outline drawing. Photocopy the furniture outlines and symbols on page 78, and cut out the shapes. Add new outlets and telephone jacks in pencil so that you can reposition them if needed.

▲ These are the five basic first-zone configurations for workstations. Beginning with one of these shapes, arrange your chair, work surfaces, and storage units.

Desktop 2'10"×7'

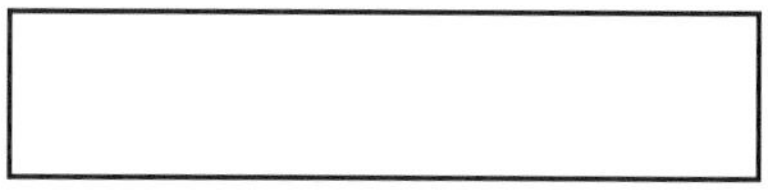

Bookcase 10×4'

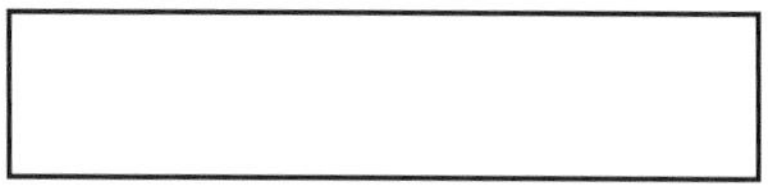

Wall-Hung Bookshelves 10×4'

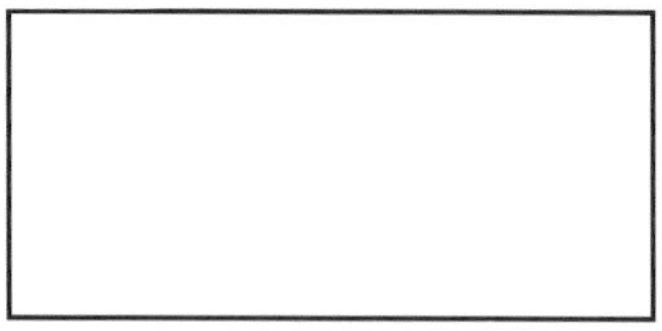

Lateral File 1'7"×3'6"

Use the graph paper, right, to make an accurate outline drawing of your office space. Include the location of doors, windows, closets, electrical outlets, and telephone jacks. Photocopy this page, then cut out the furniture shapes and position them on the outline drawing to create a layout of your office. The shapes are made to fit the scale of the graph paper, right, which is at a scale of ½ inch equals 1 foot.

△ **Telephone**

Outlet

Legal File 1'7"×2'6"

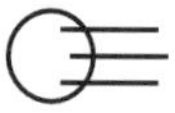

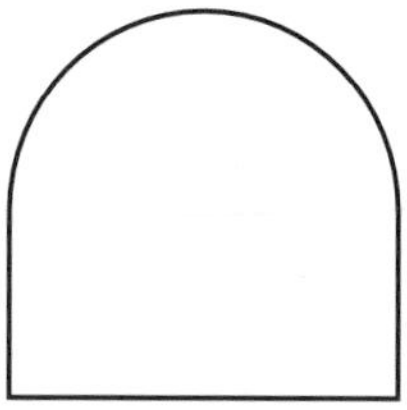

Desk Chair 2'×2'1"

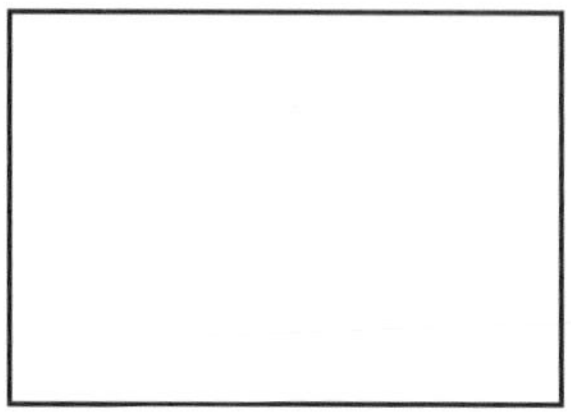

Printer Stand 2×3'

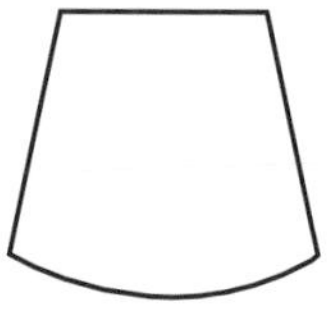

Monitor 1'2"×1' 6"

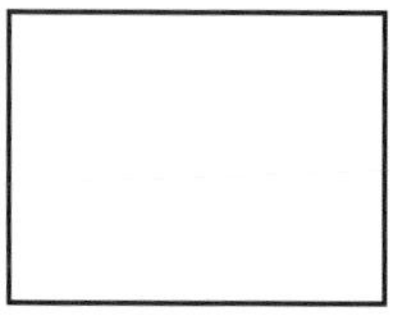

Printer 1'6"×2'

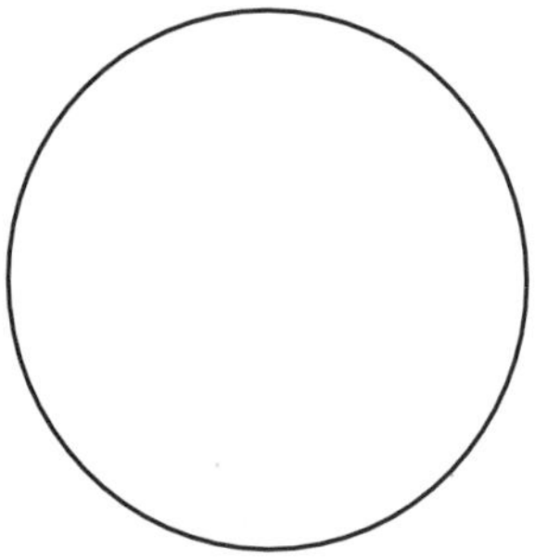

Conference Table 36" diameter

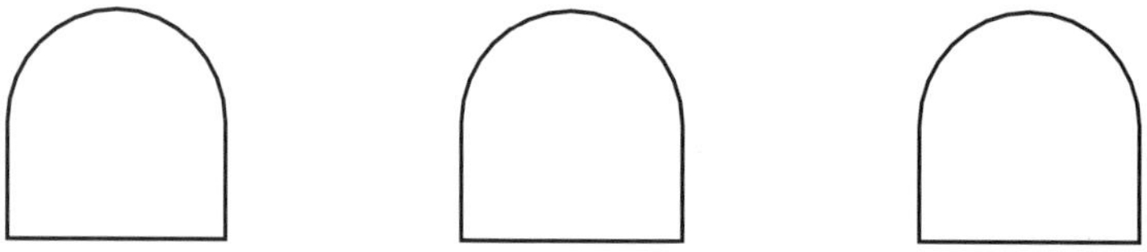

Side Chairs 1'6"×1'6"

Ergonomics and Health

Working at home often requires hours of sitting in a chair facing a computer terminal. While the situation seems harmless enough, holding your body in one position for long periods of time can strain muscles, tendons, and ligaments. It may lead to fatigue, chronic aches and pains, and even serious injury called repetitive strain injury or RSI. To avoid RSI and related health risks, it is important that your work environment—your chair, desk, computer keyboard, and monitor—be placed properly and be fitted correctly to the size of your body.

Increasingly, we are recognizing the importance of a healthy work environment. Many manufacturers now make tools and furniture that are fitted precisely to the human body. The science of designing these items is called ergonomics. Good ergonomic design reduces the risks of injury and improves productivity and well-being.

Because people come in many shapes and sizes, most ergonomically designed furniture and equipment has adjustable features. When outfitting your office, select pieces that can be raised, lowered, or tilted until they feel comfortable and fit your body. As a general rule, the more adjustable features an item has, the better the chances it will fit you correctly.

When designing an office workstation with ergonomics in mind, begin at the floor. Your feet should rest comfortably on the floor. If your legs are short, use a footrest or foot rocker. A footrest elevates your legs, reducing the pressure that the edge of your chair puts on the bottom of your thighs and improving circulation to your lower legs. A foot rocker allows you to flex your ankles, which helps prevent fatigue in leg

muscles. It also makes it easier to find a comfortable sitting position.

Good posture is important for those who work at computers. When sitting, ears, shoulders, and hips should be in vertical alignment. Keyboards and mouse pads should be at elbow level, and the arms should be bent about 90 degrees at the elbow when typing. Wrists should be straight, not bent, when fingers are on a keyboard. Your monitor should be positioned slightly below eye level, and tilted slightly away

KEYBOARD HEIGHT SHOULD BE 24" TO 27" FROM THE FLOOR.

▲ *Correct posture for working at a computer means ears, shoulders, and hips are in vertical alignment and arms are bent about 90 degrees at the elbows. The monitor screen should be 18 to 24 inches from the viewer's eyes and slightly below eye level. The keyboard should be 24 to 27 inches above the floor.*

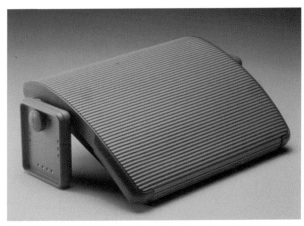

▲ *This padded footrest has four height adjustments and a nonslip surface. (From Steelcase, Inc.)*

from your line of sight so that glare is minimized.

To make your workday as comfortable and productive as possible and to minimize the chance of repetitive strain injury, try these simple techniques:

☐ Take a two-minute break at least once every half hour. Get up and walk around.

☐ Try to rotate tasks throughout the day. Follow an hour of computer work with telephone calls or reading in an easy chair.

☐ Include simple stretching exercises in your daily routine. Stand on your toes and stretch toward the ceiling for 15 seconds. Relax fully and

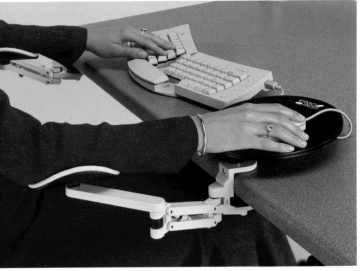

▲ *These adjustable forearm supports clamp onto most work surfaces and pivot to follow arm movements. Forearm supports reduce muscle strain associated with repetitive strain injury. (From Ergonomic Logic, Inc.)*

let your arms hang loosely at your sides. Repeat this cycle three times. Do neck rolls by gently moving your head in a circle. Make five rotations, then reverse directions.

☐ If you use a computer mouse regularly, flex your fingers frequently. Make a fist, then open your fingers as widely as you can.

☐ Use well-padded arm and wrist supports.

☐ If you need to view written material while you work at a computer, place it in front of you on a vertical copy holder. This minimizes eye movement and helps prevent eyestrain and neck strain.

☐ Place computer monitors at right angles to windows or other strong light sources to minimize glare.

Carpal Tunnel Syndrome

Carpal tunnel syndrome is a repetitive strain injury that has garnered a great deal of attention since the computer has become an integral tool of the workplace. According to the Occupational Safety and Health Administration (OSHA), more

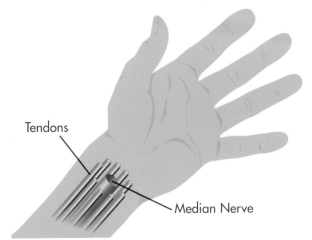

Tendons

Median Nerve

▲ *The repetitive strain injury known as carpal tunnel syndrome is related to the median nerve that runs the length of the arm and into the hand. In the wrist, the nerve is surrounded by tendons. If these tendons become irritated, they can swell and pinch the nerve.*

than half of today's workplace-related injuries are repetitive strain injuries, most often carpal tunnel syndrome.

Carpal tunnel syndrome is caused by irritation of a nerve that runs the length of the arm and into the wrist. If your hand is held at an awkward angle for long periods of time, the tendons in the wrist can become inflamed, pinching the nerve. The condition is worsened by muscle tension in the upper arm or back. Numbness, a tingling sensation, and debilitating pain can result. Occasionally, surgery is required to relieve the pressure on the nerve.

Carpal tunnel syndrome often is associated with poor posture while working with a keyboard or computer mouse. To help prevent carpal tunnel syndrome, make sure your arms and wrists are well-supported and held at the proper angle while working. Your back should be properly supported by an ergonomically designed chair, and your computer monitor should be at or just below eye level to prevent unnecessary strain to your neck and back muscles. Take frequent breaks from computer tasks and flex your arms and fingers often.

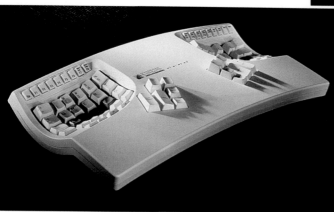

▲ Soft, foam-padded wrist rest takes the pressure off arms. The wrist rest and matching mouse pad make colorful additions to the desk. (From The Knoll Group.)

▲ This keyboard has separate concave keypads for each hand and integrated palm supports. It is curved across its width to reduce muscle tension in the wrists. (From Kinesis Corp.)

▶ Wrist pad and mouse pad are cushioned for comfort. These versions have a height adjustment. (From Steelcase, Inc.)

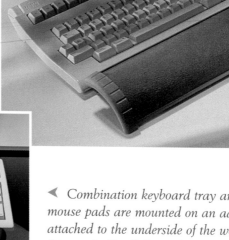

◀ Combination keyboard tray and wrist and mouse pads are mounted on an adjustable arm attached to the underside of the work surface. (From The Knoll Group.)

▲ *Wide, contoured grips filled with gel material conform to the hand and make holding these pens easy. (From Reliable Home Office.)*

▲ *This paper trimmer has a rotary blade on a steel arm and is designed to be safer than the chopping blade of traditional paper cutters. (From Reliable Home Office.)*

▲ *A low-impact spring mechanism allows light pressure to do the work with this stylish stapler. (From Office Depot.)*

▲ *This foot rest rocks up and down, allowing you to flex your feet and ankles. (From Levenger.)*

▲ *This ergonomically designed workstation has adjustable surface height, computer monitor holder, forearm supports, and chair. A telephone holder swivels for easy access. (From Ergonomic Logic, Inc.)*

Desks and Workstations

Desks and workstations come in many sizes and configurations. Some are complete with shelves, filing cabinets, computer stands, and built-in keyboard shelves. Some are ingeniously compact and mobile. Others masquerade as elegant pieces of furniture that open or unfold to reveal miniature offices. Some designs are modular, allowing you to change configurations and add shelving and storage.

Traditional desks make good administrative workstations for reading mail, writing checks, and placing telephone calls. Most desks have work surface heights 29 or 30 inches above the floor. Keyboards, however, should be 24 to 27 inches high. If you want to place a computer on your desk, the desk should have a keyboard shelf and an adjustable stand for the computer monitor. Good ergonomic designs have keyboard shelves that can raise, lower, and tilt to fit your needs.

◄ *This looks like an armoire when it is closed, above. When open, left, it reveals bookshelves, filing cabinet, room for a computer and printer, and fold-down work surface. (From Broyhill Furniture Industries, Inc.)*

► *This handsome home office features custom woodworking: a walnut desk and a wall full of matching bookshelves.*

Ready-to-assemble workstation furniture is shipped directly to the consumer in boxes. This saves money on factory assembly and inventory costs, and the savings are passed on to the buyer. You may prefer this type of furniture if you are creating a large or complex workstation. That way, everything can be carried easily into your office before it is assembled. The quality of ready-to-assemble furniture made by reputable manufacturers is usually fine, but look for companies that offer full money-back guarantees.

Some companies make mobile workstation carts designed to hold a computer and provide storage space. Mobile carts are ideal for creating an office in a small space.

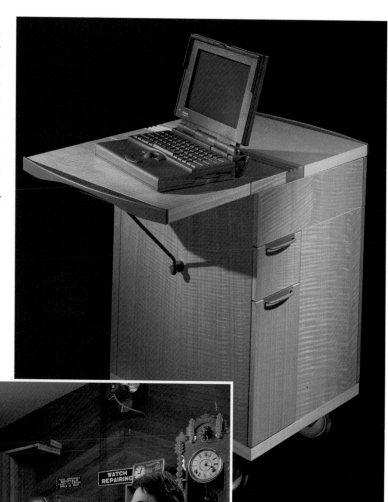

▲ *This mobile workstation is made of cherry. It has a storage compartment, a folding work surface, and oversized wheels that roll easily over different types of flooring. (From The Knoll Group.)*

◄ *This 36-inch-wide rolling computer work surface can be adjusted to a variety of heights to fit many needs. The shelves also are adjustable. (From Anthro Corp.)*

▲ *This steel-framed workstation consists of four separate pieces: a work table, a curved corner unit, a hutch, and a mobile file cabinet. The work surfaces are* *laminate. The modular design of this and similar workstations allows you to configure the size and shape to fit your office. (From Reliable Home Office.)*

Desks and Workstations

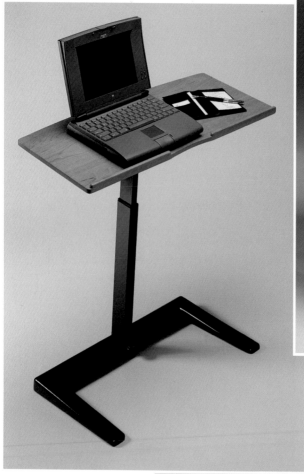

▲ This traditionally styled solid cherry desk is 43 inches wide and 24 inches deep. A concealed, pull-out tray holds the keyboard at the proper height. (From Broyhill Furniture Industries, Inc.)

▲ This small but efficient workstation features adjustable heights and a tilting work surface. Large polyethylene foot pads allow the unit to slide easily over most floor surfaces. (From Levenger.)

▶ This mobile corner workstation is 32 inches from front to back to accommodate large computer monitors. Optional wing extension units on either side increase the work surface. (From Anthro Corp.)

▲ This 8-foot-wide workstation features a desk with a pull-out keyboard tray, cabinets for storage, and a shelf for storing a computer processor on its side. A rolling file cabinet provides additional storage. (From Techline.)

▶ Although it looks like mahogany dining room furniture, this 25-inch-wide hutch holds a complete computer setup. The keyboard sits on a pull-out tray. (From Reliable Home Office.)

▲ This charming workstation is designed to look like a European baker's rack. It is 47 inches wide and features a pull-out keyboard tray. (From Reliable Home Office.)

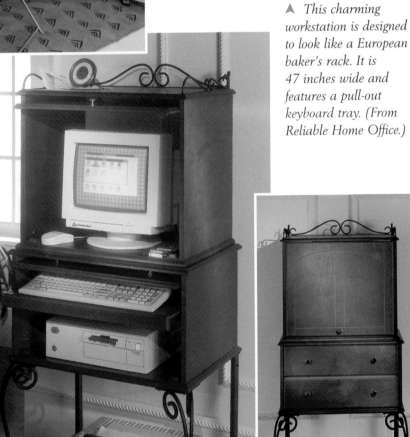

Chairs

A workstation chair is the most important piece of furniture in your home office. A properly designed chair prevents fatigue, backache, neck ache, and many of the repetitive strain injuries associated with sitting for hours at a workstation. A quality chair can determine if your day is a comfortable and productive one.

A good office chair has many adjustable features including seat height, back angle, and armrest positions. Minor changes in sitting posture help relieve the tension caused when muscles remain in the same position for long periods, and chairs with easily adjustable features can provide

vital support for your body at key points—your back, your arms, and your upper legs—throughout the day.

Today's office chairs are marvels of ergonomic engineering. A quality office chair will have a curved front or "waterfall" edge to the seat. The waterfall prevents the edge of the seat from putting pressure on the backs of your thighs, a condition that can reduce blood flow to the lower legs, causing aches and a sensation of fatigue. Armrests should be slightly curved in all

▼ *This office chair is covered in custom upholstery that gives it a comfortable at-home feel. Many manufacturers offer an array of fabrics that allow you to match your chair to your office decor.*

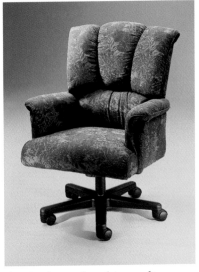

▲ *This movable lumbar support adjusts up and down until it fits your back. (From Steelcase, Inc.)*

▲ *Traditional cushion styling makes this armchair especially inviting. (From La-Z-Boy, Inc.)*

▲ *This chair has adjustable back, seat tilt, and height positions plus a sliding seat. (From The Knoll Group.)*

directions so there are no hard edges. They should be well-padded and adjustable, not only up and down but from side to side.

The human spine is slightly S-shaped, and the back of a well-designed office chair is curved to fit this part of the human anatomy. Some chair backs also flex, tilt, and adjust up and down to provide support as you change positions during the day. There are also chairs with pneumatically controlled chambers so that the shape of the backrest can be changed with the twist of a knob.

THE ADJUSTABLE OFFICE CHAIR

Ergonomic design provides adjustable features that make chairs comfortable.

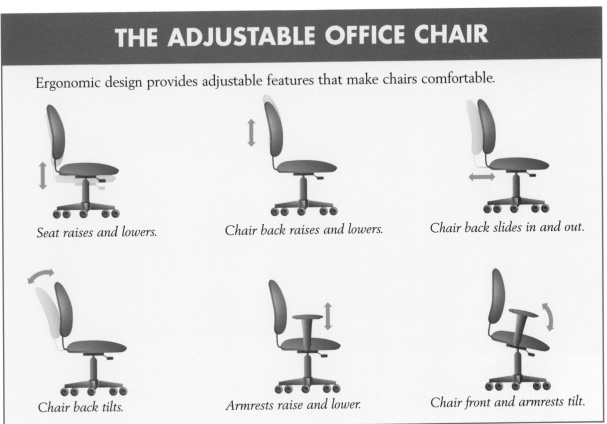

Seat raises and lowers.

Chair back raises and lowers.

Chair back slides in and out.

Chair back tilts.

Armrests raise and lower.

Chair front and armrests tilt.

Chairs

Chairs on rolling casters allow you to move about the workstation, access file drawers, and reposition yourself in front of a computer monitor. Look for a chair that is supported by a base called a five-star base—five radiating arms with casters at the ends. Only a few years ago many office chairs were manufactured with four-star bases. This configuration is not as stable as a five-star base. If you have an older four-star-type chair, it's a good idea to replace it.

Caster-type chairs will not roll easily on floors covered with carpets. If your office has carpet, consider a chair mat. Chair mats provide a smooth, durable surface for casters to roll on. They are usually clear, so the color and pattern of the carpet can show through.

If you have the space in your office, consider adding an inviting upholstered chair or recliner and placing a reading lamp nearby. Half an hour of reading, resting, or creative thinking in a comfortable chair is time well spent. Varying your work routine and changing the position of your body helps prevent muscle fatigue.

▲ *This high-backed chair comes with a headrest and many adjustable features. (From Global Industries, Inc.)*

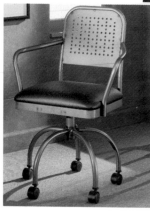

▲ *This metal chair has a padded seat. (From Reliable Home Office.)*

▲ *This sophisticated office chair is crafted with cherry wood accents and leather upholstery. It features adjustable height and back supports. (From Levenger.)*

◄ *Comfort is a priority in this home office. It features an ergonomically designed workstation chair and upholstered easy chairs with matching ottomans for relaxing and reading in style.*

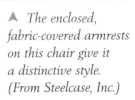

▲ *The enclosed, fabric-covered armrests on this chair give it a distinctive style. (From Steelcase, Inc.)*

▲ *Adjustable lumbar support is an option for this modern armchair. (From The Knoll Group.)*

▲ *This contemporary-styled wood guest chair has eight fabric options. (From The Knoll Group.)*

GUEST SEATING

Chairs intended for visitors don't have to be as ergonomically sophisticated as workstation chairs, but they should be inviting, comfortable pieces of furniture that make guests feel welcome. They should be lightweight so they can be moved around your office easily. If you expect visitors to your home office on a regular basis, plan for a pair of matching guest chairs.

Filing and Storage

Filing, shelving, and storage systems contribute to the efficiency and organization of your office. The best arrangements put your most frequently used items close at hand.

It's a good idea to plan for some of your storage to be flexible and able to adapt to your needs as your work load changes. Modular shelving units with adjustable shelves and small, mobile file cabinets that are easily shifted around your office are examples of flexible storage.

File Cabinets

File cabinets are made in two basic formats: vertical and lateral. Vertical file cabinets are 28 to 24 inches deep and about 15 inches wide. Cabinets for legal-sized documents are about 19 inches wide. File folders face the user as the drawer is opened. Vertical file cabinets fit well at the end of a desk or a table. Some have casters and are designed to roll underneath work surfaces.

Lateral file cabinets are 30 to 48 inches wide and 15 to 20 inches deep, and their file folders are either front- or side-facing. Lateral units are designed to be placed against walls. Both vertical and lateral cabinets are available in two- to five-drawer heights. The format you purchase should be the shape that works best with your office configuration.

File cabinets come in many styles, from sleek steel units with baked-on enamel finishes to traditional wood varieties. No matter what your personal style, select file cabinets that have top-quality drawer slides—the mechanism that holds the drawer as it is opened and closed. The best drawer slides have ball-bearing rollers, are fully extendable, and work smoothly and effortlessly even when supporting a fully loaded drawer.

Always use caution when loading file cabinets and opening drawers. Although most file cabinets remain stable when a single drawer is extended, they may tip over if two loaded drawers are opened at the same time. For safety, some file cabinets have catch mechanisms that prevent two or more drawers from being opened simultaneously. Others have counterbalance weights

▲ *This office takes advantage of available space with a built-in shelf over the door. A classic column adds a formal style.*

installed in their frames to prevent mishaps.

For added safety, it's a good idea to attach stationary file cabinets to a wall. First find a stud in the wall behind the cabinet. Remove the upper drawer and drill a hole through the back of the cabinet, aligning the hole with the stud. Then drive a wood screw through the hole into the stud. The screw must be long enough to pass through ½ inch of drywall and penetrate at least 1 inch into the stud.

Shelving

The big difference between shelves and cabinets is that everything on your shelves is also on display. Shelves look great with books, plants, family pictures, or knickknacks, but loose papers and office supplies are best stored out of sight.

Shelves come in three basic types: wall-mounted, freestanding, and built-in. Wall-mounted shelves are the least expensive option and are simple to install. Track-and-bracket wall shelving has metal tracks screwed directly to wall studs or into a solid wood backing that is attached to the studs. Brackets clip to the tracks and support shelves. The brackets are easily moved so shelves adjust to different heights.

Freestanding shelving units also are called

▲ *Custom-built undercounter cabinetry allows the computer processor, copy machine, and photo scanner to disappear at the end of the day.*

▲ *In this compact office all essential items are within easy reach of the workstation chair.*

▲ *Storage can be located outside the office. This built-in bookshelf was placed along a hallway to free up space within the home office.*

Filing and Storage 95

bookcases. Generally, bookcases come in two heights. Units with three or four shelves are 27 to 36 inches high, the same height as a desk or work surface. Bookcases 60 to 72 inches high have six or more shelves. The standard depth for shelving is about 12 inches. The advantage of freestanding shelving is that units can be repositioned whenever you want, providing greater flexibility for the design of your office.

Ready-to-assemble furniture manufacturers offer free-standing shelf units that are inexpensive and easy to put together. They may have such options as drawers and cabinet doors so that the unit can be customized. Finishes vary, but keep in mind that shelves covered with laminate veneers usually are made of particleboard. Shelves of solid wood will be stronger and more resistant to sagging over time.

For safety, it's a good idea to attach tall bookcases to the wall behind them. Some manufacturers provide a safety strap—a ribbon of tough woven nylon used to attach the top of the bookcase to a wall stud with wood screws.

Built-in shelves are usually the most expensive option. Their construction requires careful measuring and cutting to create a precise fit. Often, built-ins are trimmed with the same baseboard or crown moldings installed around the perimeter of your office. That way, the built-in unit is integrated into your home's architecture and interior design. Because built-ins are a permanent feature of your office, you should plan their appearance and location carefully.

Active Storage

Active storage is another term for the first zone storage discussed on page 74. Active storage holds items you need to access regularly throughout the day. These items should be reachable from your workstation chair. Active storage includes office supplies, such as pens, papers, and notepads, as well as frequently used reference books or files—materials and records relevant to your current work projects. Desks and workstations often provide for active storage with a shallow pencil drawer for small office supplies and a drawer for files. Small desktop shelf units and rolling file cabinets are examples of active storage that adds flexibility to your workstation.

▲ *This plastic wall organizer accepts a variety of clip-on accessories that are moveable and keep clutter off work surfaces. (From Steelcase, Inc.)*

▲ *Wall-mounted shelving rests on moveable brackets attached to steel tracks. A wide lower shelf can be used as a work surface. (From The Container Store.)*

▲ Traditional steel lateral files provide lots of storage in a small area. A laminate work surface placed on top of the cabinets makes a good workstation. (From Global Industries, Inc.)

▲ Small desktop shelf units put flexible storage within easy reach. This cherry example is 31 inches wide, 10 inches deep, and 16 inches high. (From Levenger.)

▲ These solid-wood vertical file cabinets are modular and stackable. You buy single-drawer units and create two-, three-, or four-drawer cabinets. (From Levenger.)

Staying Organized

A successful home office is one that you enjoy working in. The key to creating a successful home office is to organize it and then keep it organized with regular maintenance and periodic cleaning. A well-maintained office can increase productivity by reducing the time you spend looking for things, providing efficient ways to handle paperwork, and helping you focus on priorities.

Just because an office is neat and tidy doesn't always mean it's organized efficiently. Similarly, stacks of papers or piles of books covering a desktop aren't necessarily a sign of a hopelessly befuddled home-based worker. Each person works best under different conditions. One of the great advantages of working from home is the opportunity to create an office setup and a routine that are reflections of your personality and style. The ultimate goal should be to work as effectively as possible so stress is reduced and you are able to maximize your time outside the work environment as well.

Organization is a two-step process. The first is to provide a location for the supplies and materials essential to your work. The old adage, "A place for everything, and everything in its place," is still an excellent guiding principle. Establish defined locations for all your items, placing your most-used materials within arm's reach of your workstation chair. If at first you don't know where to put something, then take the time to invent a place for it. You should know exactly where all supplies and materials belong when it comes time to straighten up. Effective organization of your physical work space is often a learning process. Experiment until you find the locations and arrangements that work for you.

It's a good idea to have some flexible storage near your workstation. A small organizer or desktop shelf unit, a desk file drawer, or a rolling file cabinet are examples of flexible storage space. The items you place in flexible storage will change periodically as your work shifts from one project to another. When you're finished with them, the materials in your flexible storage can be returned to their more permanent locations.

Reduce clutter by removing nonessential items from the workplace. The less stuff you have to manage, the more efficient and easier to maintain your office will become. If you have knick-knacks or family mementos you want to display

▲ *This rolling metal file cabinet can be positioned next to your desk when needed, then stored across the room. (From Hold Everything.)*

▲ *This sleek metal organizer provides desktop storage for important papers. (From Atapco Office Products.)*

▲ *This wood-and-wicker shelf unit keeps desktop clutter out of sight. (From Hold Everything.)*

▲ *This home office is a study in organization, thanks to a floor-to-ceiling storage unit directly behind the* *desk. Personal items give the space character, yet essentials are close at hand.*

in your office, have a special shelf just for them.

The second step toward organization is periodic maintenance and cleaning. Set aside an hour or two each week to go through papers, materials, and supplies that may have accumulated on your work surfaces and return them to their proper locations. You'll be surprised how many things have made a home for themselves on your desk simply because you've gotten used to seeing them. Throw away extraneous papers, envelopes, and memos. If you can't bear to part with something because you "may need it someday," then file it. You may never refer to it again, but at least it will be out of sight. Two or three times each

year, purge your filing system of unwanted or out-of-date items.

Clean your office once each week. Vacuum floors, dust shelves and equipment, straighten up bookshelves, and empty wastebaskets. If you use a computer, clean your monitor glass with a non-ammonia glass cleaner.

Some home office workers may find it a challenge to adhere to a maintenance routine, but the results are worth the effort. A clean and organized work space helps streamline your work load, reduces the stress of looking for misplaced items, and enables you to concentrate better on the tasks at hand.

Establishing Harmony

Give your home office personality and character through color, plants, antiques, and window treatments.

▲ *Tall, 12-foot ceilings prevent this small 7x11-foot office from feeling too cramped. Simple, streamlined furnishings give the room a relaxed, uncluttered appearance.*

One of the most enjoyable aspects of making a home office is adding the personal touches—the colors, furnishings, fabrics, and accessories—that reflect your taste and individuality. You can have your office as businesslike or as playful as you want, but the result should be nondistracting surroundings that encourage creativity and your best work.

Your home office is part of your domestic environment and should have visual harmony with the other areas of your home. This is especially true if your office or studio shares space with another room, such as a bedroom or family room. Select colors and furnishings that complement the decorative scheme of your house. If your home is furnished with country antiques, for example, establishing a modern white-and-chrome office in the middle of it probably would be harsh and unsettling.

Just as effective organization depends in part on reducing office clutter, you should try to reduce visual clutter as well. Too many different colors, patterns of fabric and wallpaper, and styles of furniture will tend to produce a distracting background. It's likely you already have a number of elements, such as computers, office equipment, bulletin boards, and supplies, that contribute to visual clutter. Try to balance the many disparate elements by selecting a basic design motif for your office—a few choice pieces of Mission-style furniture, for example—then add rugs, artwork, and accessories that build on that theme. Avoid the temptation to personalize your office with an overflow of mementos, souvenirs, or children's artwork. Your goal is to create a soothing yet interesting space that is conducive to working.

Some design decisions, such as floor finishes, wall colors, and window treatments, are best made prior to furnishing your office. Others, such as buying a special antique piece or adding unique accessories, can be made after your office layout is complete and the furniture is installed. Don't hesitate to amend your office if you feel the changes will help you concentrate on your work more effectively.

▲ *Eccentric furnishings with bold colors and patterns give this writing nook a comfortable charm. Bright grosgrain ribbon was glued to window casings and over base moldings for an added splash of color.*

▲ *Stucco walls provide just the right rustic touch for an office that includes rugged oak Mission-style* *furniture and Western-style accessories. Install special wall finishes before furnishing your office.*

Color

Color is a powerful design tool. It not only influences the look of a room and all the furnishings, it also can affect the mood of people inside the room. For an office, it's important to select a color that is a good balance—one that provides a soothing, stress-reducing background yet one that energizes your creativity.

Everyone responds to colors differently. For some, bright red is stimulating, for others, it's simply unsettling. Some people think black makes a sophisticated statement, others think dark hues are depressing. When considering colors for your home office, carefully evaluate your preferences.

For most people, color decisions are challenging. If you're not sure what colors will look and feel best, look through books or magazines that feature home interiors with color combinations you like. Pay attention not only to wall and trim colors but to furnishings, carpets, rugs, and artwork. You may decide that what attracts you isn't just a color but the look of natural wood. If so, you might want to include natural wood floors and plenty of wood furniture.

As you plan the colors of your office, keep in mind these guidelines:

☐ Color and light are in direct relationship to each other. Warm hues, such as rose, peach, and ocher, are naturally bright "sunshine" colors. Cooler hues, such as blue and violet, are "shade"

▲ *Sophisticated use of color is evident in this home office. Dark green walls and plum-colored furniture* *upholstery are set off by a white desk and neutral-toned carpet.*

▲ *Pink-and-white patterned wallpaper and upholstery help make this spacious office attractive and stimulating. Roll-up matchstick shades control window light intensity.*

colors. If your office receives a great deal of sunlight throughout the year, you might want to compensate with soothing shade colors. Similarly, a dark basement or north-facing room might benefit from the warming effects of sunshine hues.

☐ Dark colors absorb light, pale colors reflect it. If light is important to you or your work—as with architects who require lots of ambient light—you'll want to avoid dark-colored walls. If you like dark, rich colors, you'll need to compensate for the light-absorbing qualities of your scheme with adequate sources of daylight and artificial light.

☐ Lighter hues create a feeling of expansion, dark colors convey a sense of intimacy and enclosure. A small room can be made to feel larger with light colors, but carefully consider your personal preferences. If you like the idea of a cozy office, you might want to enhance the sensation by painting your already-small office with medium or dark colors.

☐ If you like soft pastel wall colors, emphasize them with white. Using white for trim, passage doors, and ceilings will help you get the most impact from pastels.

Antiques

Buying antique furniture is a great way to personalize your office. Antiques lend warmth and character to interiors, provide visual interest, and prevent home office work spaces from becoming too businesslike. Many period pieces are finely made and unmatched in quality. Others are simply fun and funky. Whatever your preference, your antiques should blend with the overall design of your office.

Shopping for bargains is part of the enjoyment of looking for antique furnishings. Flea markets, auctions, and second-hand stores are all good places to find unusual pieces at good prices. If you're looking for something specific, familiarize yourself with current prices and styles before you go hunting so you'll know a bargain when you spot it. There are many guidebooks available at bookstores and libraries that offer information on antique prices and quality.

Generally, it's not recommended that you buy an antique chair for your main workstation chair if you plan to sit in it for long periods each day. Most antique chairs are not ergonomically correct and they may contribute to muscle aches and other discomforts. However, antiques can substitute for just about any other kind of office furniture. You might find an antique piece whose original use is unknown. A little imagination may be all you need to turn it into a bookshelf, magazine rack, or bookend.

Here are some general types of antiques that often work well in the home office:

☐ Commercial shelf units and display cabinets. Many older examples have drawers or pull-out shelves that provide extra storage.

☐ Wooden desks or farm tables. Old desks are a favorite way to introduce character into your work space. Farm tables are increasingly rare and expensive but make wonderful work surfaces. Check to make sure all drawers are intact and working properly. Look for desks made of solid wood—desks with damaged veneered surfaces can be found at good prices, but veneer is difficult and costly to repair. The damage may be an indication that the veneer glue is failing. Unless you can live with the imperfections or unless the veneer is in pristine condition, avoid veneered desks.

☐ File cabinets. Traditional file cabinets from the 1920s were made of oak with brass trim and details. They are favorites of antique collectors, and it's difficult to find bargains. Old oak file cabinets may cost as much or more than their modern counterparts of the same size and capacity. To find bargains, you may

▲ *This 70-year-old oak file cabinet has a rich golden patina that comes with age.*

▲ *An exquisite 18th-century writing desk features a top made of finely figured walnut veneer. The best veneered antiques are free of warps and chipping.*

▲ *Antiques abound in this cozy writer's corner. The bookshelf is fashioned from the wooden hull of an English racing shell. Additional storage is provided by a* 19th-century, wall-hung pine shelf unit with a row of small drawers across the bottom that hold miscellaneous office supplies.

have to purchase damaged examples and have them repaired. The drawers of older file cabinets will have to be fitted with steel rails that allow them to accept today's hanging file systems.

□ Small boxes or apothecary chests. You can use small wooden or tin boxes as desktop storage for pens, computer disks, and other office supplies. You'll probably find old boxes of odd shapes and fine character at good prices. Apothecary chests, which typically have many small useful drawers in a single unit, are prized by antique collectors and priced accordingly.

Window Treatments

Window treatments play an essential role in interior design and in regulating the amount of daylight that enters the home office. Controlling daylight keeps glare off your computer monitor, reduces eyestrain, and contributes to a healthy work environment. For reading or other visual tasks, an office should remain open to daylight.

Window treatments also contribute to privacy. You might like the look of lacy curtains, but if you like privacy, too, add fold-up blinds or rolling window shades. There may be times when you want to limit your own view of the outside so you can concentrate better. Large fabric treatments, such as floor-to-ceiling draperies, are useful for controlling daylight. They also reduce outside noises transmitted through windows and absorb ambient noise within the office.

The style of window treatment is a matter of personal taste. It can be subtle or a dramatic expression of your personality. No matter what they look like, however, they should allow full control of daylight. Often, decorative window treatments can be used in combination with shades, blinds, or shutters. If you like fabric treatments, such as swags, valances, or jabots, be sure to install miniblinds or shades inside the window sash to control light. Decorative shades are a good compromise, providing light control and complementing the design of your office interiors.

▲ *The jagged linen valance features a dark trim in a color echoed in the piping on the slipcovered desk chair. Decorative gold stars and accessories add sparkle to an otherwise neutral scheme.*

▶ *An elegant swag and jabot treatment in a whimsical fabric makes a bold color statement in this home work center. Miniblinds behind the treatment control light intensity.*

▲ *Heavy fabric shades located behind a simple valance provide excellent control of daylight in this window-filled office. The fabric shades add subtle colors to the interior scheme.*

Plants

Consider plants to be an essential component of the interior design of your office. They add natural forms and colors that have been associated with enhanced creativity and reduced stress, and they complement any design scheme. Plants produce oxygen and have the ability to remove carbon dioxide and certain airborne pollutants, an especially important quality in northern climates where winter demands that windows be closed for many months each year. If space is a problem, plant hangers can be attached to ceiling joists.

There are many kinds of indoor house plants that tolerate a variety of growing conditions, and many varieties have the ability to adapt somewhat to the amount of light, heat, and water they are given. Most plants will stand somewhat higher temperatures than recommended, as long as they are compensated with higher levels of humidity. In general, it is better to underwater indoor plants rather than overwater.

Plants for Basement Offices

Basement offices, which are often without the benefit of much natural light or ventilation and can feel isolated, benefit from the positive psychological effect of green living plants. But basements offer some of the most challenging growing conditions. A good solution is to grow plants under artificial light. Properly set up, artificial light is an effective substitute for natural light.

Fluorescent lights are the best and most economical source of light for plants. They burn at a relatively cool temperature so the danger of scorching plant leaves is minimal. Select a two-tube fluorescent light fixture slightly larger than the plant containers or the surface that holds your plants. Install a daylight-type tube in one holder and a natural-white tube in the other. This combination provides the full spectrum of light that most plants require. The light source should be about 1 foot above the tallest plants. Smaller plants can be set on stands to raise their tops to the correct distance.

It is best to place your light source on an electronic timer that automatically turns the unit on and off. In conditions of extremely low natural light, plants should receive 12 to 14 hours of artificial light each day. Flowering plants, such as African violets (Saintpaulia), should receive 16 to 18 hours of light each day.

When selecting plants for basement offices, try to choose those that thrive in low-temperature conditions because most basements are consistently cool.

EASY-CARE PLANT VARIETIES

For bright light conditions
Veitch screw pine (Pandanus veitchii)
Earth star plant (Cryptanthus bivittatus)
Wax begonia (Begonia semperflorens-cultorum)
Lemon geranium (Pelargonium crispum "Variegatum")
Painted nettle (Coleus blumei)
Impatiens (Impatiens walleriana)
Cape ivy (Senecio macroglossus)
Wandering Jew (Zebrina pendula)
Swedish ivy (Plectranthus australis)

For medium or filtered light conditions
English ivy (Hedera helix)
Spider plant (Chlorophytum comosum)
Kangaroo vine (Cissus antarctica)
Grape ivy (Cissus rhombifolia)
Spotted laurel (Aucuba japonica)
Florist's chrysanthemum (Chrysanthemum morifolium)
German violet (Exacum affine)
Ponytail (Beaucarnea recurvata)

For low light conditions
Boston fern (Nephrolepis exaltata)
Burgundy philodendron (Philodendron)
Swiss cheese plant (Monstera deliciosa)
Heartleaf philodendron (Philodendron scandens)
Delta maidenhair fern (Adiantum raddiantum)
Prayer plant (Maranta leuconeura erthroneura)

◀ If you have the space, plants make nice additions to work surfaces, but make sure plant maintenance doesn't jeopardize sensitive equipment.

▲ Indoor trees, such as this weeping fig (Ficus benjamina), *look great in large rooms. They can grow more than 6 feet tall. Add flowers to brighten your day.*

MANUFACTURERS

Anthro Corp.
10450 SW. Manhasset Dr.
Tulatin, OR 97062
800/325-0045

Atapco Office Products
12312 Olive Blvd.
Suite 400
St. Louis, MO 63141

Balt, Inc.
201 N. Crockett St.
Cameron, TX 76520
800/733-3532

Broyhill Furniture Industries, Inc.
1 Broyhill Park
Lenoir, NC 28633
704/758-3111

Ergonomic Logic, Inc.
205 Vista Blvd.
#101
Sparks, NV 89434
800/527-6600

Ethan Allen
Ethan Allen Dr.
P.O. Box 1966
Danbury, CT 06811-1966
800/228-9229

Global Industries, Inc.
17 W. Stowe Rd.
Marlton, NJ 08053
800/220-1900

Haworth, Inc.
One Haworth Center
Holland, MI 49423-9576
800/393-3000

Herman Miller for the Home
855 E. Main Ave.
Zeeland, MI 49464-0302
800/646-4400

Kinesis Corp.
22121 17th Ave.
Suite 112
Bothell, WA 98021
800/454-6374

The Knoll Group
105 Wooster St.
New York, NY 10012
800/445-5045

La-Z-Boy, Inc.
1284 N. Telegraph Rd.
Monroe, MI 48162
313/241-2105

Levenger
420 S. Congress Ave.
Del Ray Beach, FL 33445-4696
800/544-0880

▲ *This workstation setup features white laminate maple veneer doors and drawers. There's plenty of storage space and a corner desk with a pull-out keyboard tray. A mobile file cabinet on casters fits under the desk. (From Techline.)*

Steelcase, Inc.
P.O. Box 1967
Grand Rapids, MI 49501-1967
800/333-9939

Techline
500 S. Division St.
Waunakee, WI 53597
800/666-0947

Waldmann Lighting
9 W. Century Dr.
Wheeling, IL 60090
800/634-0007

MAIL ORDER

The Container Store
214/654-4959

Crate & Barrel
800/323-5461

Hold Everything
800/421-2264

Office Depot
800/685-8800

OfficeMax
800/788-8080

Paper Direct
800/272-7377

Pottery Barn
800/922-5507

Reliable Home Office
800/869-6000

Staples
800/333-3330

▲ *This wood desk, made of solid ash and hardwood veneers, has everything for today's office, including pull-out keyboard and mouse trays and a compartment for a computer processor. (From Broyhill Furniture Industries, Inc.)*

INFORMATION

American Association of Home Based Business
P.O. Box 10023
Rockville, MD 20849
800/447-9710

American Institute of Architects
1735 New York Ave., NW
Washington, DC 20006
202/626-7300

American Society of Interior Designers
608 Massachusetts Ave., SE
Washington, DC 20021

Index

Numbers in **bold** indicate pages with photographs.

U.S. Units to Metric Equivalents		
To convert from	Multiply by	To get
Inches	25.4	Millimetres (mm)
Inches	2.54	Centimetres (cm)
Feet	30.48	Centimetres (cm)
Feet	0.3048	Metres (m)
Cubic Feet	28.316	Litres (l)

Metric Units to U.S. Equivalents		
To convert from	Multiply by	To get
Millimetres	0.0394	Inches
Centimetres	0.3937	Inches
Centimetres	0.0328	Feet
Metres	3.2808	Feet
Litres	0.0353	Cubic Feet